TEXTBOOK

Conveyancing

Second Edition

EDITOR: ANDREW WALKER
LLB, LLM, Solicitor

OLD BAILEY PRESS

OLD BAILEY PRESS
200 Greyhound Road, London W14 9RY

First Published 1997
Second edition 2000

© Old Bailey Press Ltd 2000

ISBN 1 85836 361 6

British Library Cataloguing-in-Publication.
A CIP Catalogue record for this book is available from the British Library.

Acknowledgement
The publishers and author would like to thank the Incorporated Council of Law Reporting for England and Wales for kind permission to reproduce extracts from the Weekly Law Reports, and Butterworths for their kind permission to reproduce extracts from the All England Law Reports.

The Standard Conditions of Sale (3rd edition 1995) are reproduced by kind permission of the Law Society of England and Wales and the Solicitors' Law Stationery Society Limited, for educational purposes only. Crown copyright material is reproduced with the kind permission of the Controller of Her Majesty's Stationery Office.

Printed and bound in Great Britain

Contents

iv   *Contents*

Preface

Old Bailey Press textbooks are written specifically for students. Whatever their course, they will find our books clear and concise, providing comprehensive and up-to-date coverage. Written by specialists in their field, our textbooks are reviewed and updated on a regular basis.

This edition deals with the conveyancing implications of recent statutes, including the Trusts of Land and Appointment of Trustees Act 1996, the Land Registration Act 1997 and the Trustee Delegation 1999. Recent cases include *Target Holdings* v *Priestley* and *Yaxley* v *Gotts & Gotts* (the effect of s2 of the Law of Property (Miscellaneous Provisions) Act 1989) and *Freeguard* v *Rogers* and *Alan Wibberley Building Ltd* v *Insley* (the description of property and interpretation of documents).

The law is as stated on 30 June 2000.

Table of Cases

Table of Statutes

Abbreviations

The following statutes, rules and conditions, and their abbreviations, are referred to in this book:

LRA	Land Registration Act 1925
LPA	Law of Property Act 1925
LCA	Land Charges Act 1972
TOLATA	Trusts of Land and Appointment of Trustees Act 1996
LRR	Land Registration Rules 1925
SC	Standard Conditions of Sale (Third Edition) 1995

1

Introduction and Overview

1.1 Introduction

1.2 An overview of a typical transaction

1.1 Introduction

The study of conveyancing is unlike most other subjects studied by a law student, as it is primarily the study of a particular transaction. It is usually described as being the creation and transfer of interests in land. The commonest transaction is the sale of a fee simple, but it can also involve other transactions – in particular the creation of mortgages, the creation of leases and the transfer of leases. The basic transaction which will be examined in this book is the transfer of a fee simple but other issues will be addressed as and when appropriate. The study of conveyancing assumes and builds on a knowledge of land law; it should not be forgotten that one objective, if not the principle objective, of the 1925 legislation was to simplify conveyancing.

A normal conveyancing transaction involves a two-stage process. There is firstly the contract, which defines the transaction which the parties are to carry out. In its simplest terms the contract states that the seller will on completion day transfer the property described in the contract to the purchaser, and on the same day the purchaser will pay to the seller the purchase price. On completion the property will be transferred to the purchaser. Completion is when the transaction defined in the contract is carried out, and it should be emphasised that it is the transaction created by the contract, nothing more and nothing less, which is carried out on completion. The contract is therefore the central document in the transaction as it sets out what the parties have to do, and what the parties have to do is what the contract states.

The legal provisions applicable to a conveyancing transaction comes from various sources:

1. statute;
2. case law;
3. contractual conditions:
   a) open contract rules;
   b) standard conditions;
   c) special conditions;

4. practice of conveyancing lawyers.

The open contract rules are those contractual provisions which will be implied into a contract if the parties do not themselves make express provision for that matter in the contract, and they may be laid down either by statute or case law. It is not usual to rely on the open contract position and invariably the parties will make their own provisions by means of contractual conditions.

There have over many years been various versions of standard conditions of sale. These were produced to reflect the current practice and were incorporated into a contract by reference. There were a variety of sets of conditions of sale – for example, the National Conditions of Sale, the Law Society's Conditions of Sale, and many local law societies also had their own conditions. These were standardised and now the operative set of conditions of sale is the Standard Conditions of Sale, 3rd edition 1995: see Appendix 6. Where a contract incorporates the Standard Conditions they will all apply unless expressly excluded or modified. In addition to standard conditions, there will also be special conditions which are contractual terms which the parties have negotiated and which apply to their transaction only.

1.2 An overview of a typical transaction

The traditional sequence of events is as follows. Once a sale has been negotiated, the first step is for the seller to prepare the draft contract. This will be prepared by reference to the documents of title (title deeds if the land is unregistered or land registry entries if the title is registered) and will describe the parties, the property and the contractual terms. In most cases the contract will incorporate the Standard Conditions of Sale. The draft contract is sent to the buyer for him to consider, comment on and amend. The draft will then be returned to the seller and this process continues until there is an agreed form of contract. The basic principle in conveyancing is caveat emptor – let the buyer beware – and it is up to the buyer to ensure that he is satisfied with the property. There is no general duty of disclosure imposed on the seller. The buyer will therefore have to make preliminary searches and investigations. He will undertake various searches in public registers – in particular a local search which is a search of the local land charges registry kept by local authorities under the Local Land Charges Act 1975. He will also make inquiries of the local authority which will reveal matters affecting the property but which are not local land charges. This is done by using a form which has been agreed between the Law Society and the local authorities. A local search and inquiries of the local authority have to be done whether the land is registered or unregistered. If the land is unregistered an index map search at the Land Registry should be done. Also, where appropriate, mining searches and commons and village green searches should be done. The buyer should also make pre-contract enquiries of the seller, asking about matters relating to the property which will be within the seller's knowledge, and a buyer should also have a survey done to satisfy himself as to the physical condition of the property. When all matters have been satisfactorily dealt with both parties sign the contract and contracts are exchanged. The contract must contain all the terms of the transaction, including the completion date. It is normal for each party to sign one copy of the contract and then to exchange them, with the result that the seller holds the copy signed by the buyer and the buyer the copy signed by the seller. There is no reason why both parties should not sign the same document, but the practice is that they do not and that identical signed copies are exchanged. Only on exchange of contracts does a legally binding transaction come into existence and until then either party can withdraw without penalty. The buyer normally pays a deposit on exchange. The seller then provides the buyer with evidence of title – in registered land office copy entries and in unregistered land either an abstract of title (a typed summary of the deeds) or an epitome (a summary of the deeds, accompanied by photocopies). This process whereby the seller proves that he has a good title is called deduction of title. In unregistered land he has to provide evidence that he and his predecessors have been in occupation for at least 15 years. The buyer then has to investigate the title, which involves checking the evidence and raising queries in relation to those matters about which he is not satisfied, called requisitions on title.

If the evidence which the seller provides is not adequate, or not in accordance with the contract, then the buyer may contend the seller is in breach and refuse to complete. If however the evidence is satisfactory, matters can proceed. The buyer drafts the transfer deed – traditionally a conveyance if the land is unregistered, a transfer if it is registered. He supplies copies to the seller who has to approve it and return one copy to the buyer. The buyer then engrosses the purchase deed – ie types up the final copy which will be the copy the parties sign. The buyer signs the purchase deed which is then sent to the seller for signature in readiness for completion. The buyer then has to carry out pre-completion searches. If the title to the land is unregistered, then a search in the Land Charges Registry needs to be done; if the title is registered an official search of the Land Registry is undertaken. Completion then takes place. The buyer checks the original title deeds to ensure that they are in accordance with the abstract and pays over the balance of the purchase price. The purchase deed is then dated and handed to the purchaser, together with any other deeds and documents. The buyer then has to pay any stamp duty payable. The stamp duty position always needs to be considered. If a document is not stamped it cannot be produced as evidence in any legal proceedings, and the Land Registry will not deal with a document which should have been stamped but which has not been. If the land is registered the buyer has to apply to register the transfer. If the land is unregistered then there will have to be an application for first registration.

The above is the traditional approach and it will be noted that the sequence is contract – evidence of title – completion. The contract set out what the seller was to do, and only after both parties were committed, ie after exchange of contract, was evidence of title supplied by the seller to the buyer. This was cumbersome and time-consuming and so in the late 1980s the Law Society introduced the Conveyancing Protocol designed to speed matters up. There have been various modifications and the version currently in use is that published in 1995. The Protocol has to be adopted by the parties, and in many respects it set out what conveyancing solicitors were already doing. The main objective is to make more information available to the buyer as early as possible in the transaction. This is achieved by the seller preparing a pre-contract package, containing the following:

1. draft contract;
2. evidence of title – either abstract/epitome or office copy entries;
3. seller's property information form – a standard form containing basic information, in many respects replies to standard preliminary inquiries;
4. fixtures and fittings list;
5. copies of documents such as planning permissions, building regulations approval, guarantees for damp-proofing timber treatment, etc.

Compared to the traditional practice much more information is made available at the outset, in particular the evidence of title. This has the effect of making the pre-contract stage much more important. Those matters which would in the past have been dealt with after exchange of contracts by requisitions on title are now dealt with by means of inquiries at the pre-contract stage. In the past problems arose because only when contracts had been exchanged would the buyer see the evidence of title, and if there were problems the buyer would have to claim the problem was such as to justify a failure to complete. Now if there is a problem with the title contracts will not be exchanged until all outstanding matters have been resolved. It should be noted that even where the Protocol as such is not being used, the practice these days is for much of the above information to be made available to the buyer before contract.

Many of the legal principles and stages in the transaction were developed in relation to the old system when issues of title were dealt with after the contract was concluded, whereas the modern practice is not the same. Nevertheless, it is still important to separate issues of title from other more general matters relating to the property.

2

Land Registration

2.1 Introduction

The traditional method of land ownership in England and Wales has been with unregistered title in which good title is proved by producing the deeds and proving possession for at least 15 years. One of the innovations of the 1925 legislation was the introduction of a comprehensive system of land registration. Registration of title has gradually been extended and, although much property is now registered, a considerable amount still remains unregistered.

The governing statute is the Land Registration Act (LRA) 1925 and the Land Registration Rules (LRR) 1925 made under it which deal with issues of detail and the working of the Land Registry.

The Land Registry consists of the Registry in London and a number of district land registries around the country. Each district land registry deals with land in designated counties. Inquiries concerning land in a particular area must be addressed to the relevant district land registry. At the Land Registry there are kept, inter alia, the registers of title and an index map which shows the extent of land the title to which is registered.

2.2 First registration of title

The scheme of land registration contained in the LRA could best be described as

5

'creeping.' One of the essential concepts is that of first registration of title, which is the process when the title to land is converted from unregistered to registered. There are two sorts of first registration of title – compulsory and voluntary.

Compulsory first registration

Before compulsory first registration is applicable to a piece of land, the area in which the land is situated has to have been designated an area of compulsory first registration. This was done gradually over the years, as areas were designated compulsory areas. On the first of a designated series of transactions after the land has been designated as being in a compulsory area there has to be an application for first registration of title. Since 1 December 1990 the whole of England and Wales has been designated a compulsory area and, as the whole of England and Wales is now a compulsory area, the first designated transaction will now trigger compulsory first registration.

Under s123 LRA (as substituted by the Land Registration Act 1997) an application for first registration of title has to be made when one of the following occurs:

1. conveyance on sale of the fee simple;
2. the grant of a lease for a term of more than 21 years;
3. the assignment on sale of an existing lease with more than 21 years left to run;
4. a deed of gift;
5. a conveyance or assignment not on sale but for consideration;
6. assents;
7. vesting assents and vesting deeds affecting settled land;
8. exchanges with no payment of equality money, including property taken in exchange by developers;
9. conveyances and assignments of onerous property (eg polluted land);
10. conveyances and assignments in pursuance of court orders;
11. first mortgages secured by deposit of title deeds of a fee simple or lease with more than 21 years left to run.

The first three listed were the original triggers contained in the LRA; the remainder were added by the Land Registration Act 1997 which came into force on 1 April 1998.

Within two months of any of the above an application for first registration of title has to be lodged at the appropriate district land registry. The application must be lodged with two months of completion, although the registrar can, and normally does, extend the period. If an application for first registration of a disposition transferring a legal estate is not submitted within the two-month period, the sanction is that at the end of the two-month period the legal estate reverts to the transferor, who will hold it as a bare trustee for the transferee until the disposition is registered. If the transaction is one which grants a legal estate or creates a legal mortgage and there is a failure to register the disposition within the two-month period the disposition takes effect as if it were a contract to grant the estate or create the charge made for valuable consideration. This provision takes effect whether or not the requirements of s2 Law of Property (Miscellaneous Provisions) Act 1989 are satisfied. If the period is extended by the Registrar then from the date of the order extending the period the legal estate or interest will revive. The application must be made by the person who is entitled to the legal estate transferred or created by the transactions contained in (1) to (10). In relation to (11) the application must be made by the estate owner of the estate charged, ie the mortgagor. The applicant must bear the costs of the application.

Voluntary first registration

An application for first registration is compulsory if one of those triggers set out at (1) – (11) above occurs. It is also possible to apply for voluntary first registration of title at any time, and in an attempt to encourage registration a reduced fee is payable on an application for voluntary first registration.

The application

An application for first registration is made by completing the relevant application form and sending to the Land Registry all deeds and documents relating to the property. The Land Registry investigates the title by making the same inquiries and adopting the same approach as a competent conveyancing solicitor, and is in effect in the same position as a willing and prudent purchaser. This means that minor defects and problems which a competent conveyancer would ignore will also be ignored by the Land Registry. There is a statutory exception to this, however. Where a tenant of a local authority or other public body exercises his right to buy under statute, the evidence of title is simply a certificate of title provided by the seller which is accepted by the Land Registry.

Caution against first registration

Any person who claims an interest in unregistered land of such a nature that he is entitled to object to first registration may lodge a caution against first registration. If such a caution is lodged, the cautioner must be given notice of an application for first registration and is entitled to object. The registration cannot proceed until he has been given this opportunity. In practice, a purchaser will carry out an index map search early in the transaction and the existence of any caution will be revealed. Thus, in most cases the issue of such a caution will be resolved well before an application for registration is submitted.

2.3 Registration of title

An estate in land may be registered with one of four classes of title. The relevant estate – either the fee simple or term of years with more than 21 years left to run – will be registered in its own right with a unique title number. These two estates are the subject of substantive registration, ie each has its own title. No other estate or interest can be registered in its own right but will have to be registered against the title which it affects.

There are four possible titles – absolute, possessory, qualified and good leasehold. The first three can apply to both freehold or leasehold; the last can obviously only apply to leaseholds.

Absolute title

Freehold
The effect of registration of a freehold with absolute title is set out in s5 LRA. Registration with absolute title vests in the proprietor an estate in fee simple in possession in the land together with all rights and privileges belonging to the land and subject to:

1. the incumbrances and other entries appearing on the register;
2. any overriding interests;
3. if the first proprietor is not entitled to the land for his own benefit, eg he is a trustee, as between himself and the person entitled to the minor interests, any minor interests of such persons of which he has notice.

but free of all other estates and interests.

The above are the only matters which can affect the proprietor's title. The register is definitive in relation to matters contained in it even if it is wrong. If there is an error, then the state of the register is determinative unless and until the register is rectified.

Leasehold
The effect of registration of a leasehold with absolute title is set out in s9 LRA.

Registration with absolute title vests the lease in the proprietor subject to those matters referred to in (1) to (3) above relating to freehold land and also subject to all express and implied covenants, obligations and liabilities affecting the registered land, ie subject to the terms of the lease and also subject to any matters registered against the landlord's title, but again free of any other matters. Registration with absolute leasehold title is confirmation that the lease was validly granted. In order to obtain registration with absolute title, under s8 LRA evidence of the freehold title and any superior lease must also be produced to the Registrar and approved. (If the superior titles are registered then absolute title will be granted as the Registrar will already have approved the superior titles when they were registered.)

Good leasehold title

This obviously only applies to leases. The effect of registration is dealt with in s10 LRA. Registration with good leasehold vests the lease in the proprietor subject to the same matters as absolute leasehold, but it does not affect the enforcement of any matter affecting the right of the lessor to grant the lease, ie it does not guarantee that the lease was validly granted. Good leasehold will be granted when the lessee cannot produce the evidence of the superior titles required under s8 for registration with absolute leasehold title. As will be seen in Chapter 14 (see section 14.2), in unregistered conveyancing a prospective lessee is not entitled in the absence of any special condition to call for evidence of the landlord's title. This provision mirrors that.

Possessory title

A person may be registered with a possessory title if he is in possession and his title is based on adverse possession or he cannot produce the evidence of title which would normally be required for him to be registered with absolute title.

Under s6 LRA registration with possessory title to a freehold vests the fee simple in the proprietor subject to those matters which affect absolute title (above). However, such registration does not affect the enforcement of any matter affecting the estate which was in existence at the time of first registration.

In relation to leaseholds, under s11 LRA registration with a possessory title vests the lease in the proprietor subject to those matters which affect absolute leasehold title, but does not affect the enforcement of any matter, whether relating to the lessor's estate or otherwise, which adversely affects the proprietor's title and which was in existence at the time of first registration.

The effect of both of these provisions is that there are excluded from the effect of registration any matters affecting the land which were in existence at the time of first registration.

It is in relation to titles obtained by adverse possession that a significant difference between registered and unregistered land can be seen. Under s15 Limitation Act 1980 no action shall be brought for the recovery of land after 12 years have passed since the cause of action accrued. Under s17, at the end of the 12-year period the title of the original owner is extinguished. Under s75 LRA however, where title to land is registered and the 12-year period has passed the proprietor's rights are not extinguished under the Limitation Act but the proprietor is deemed to hold the estate upon trust for the person who has acquired a title by adverse possession.

In unregistered land, if a lessee loses his title by adverse possession to a squatter who acquires a title by adverse possession, a surrender by the original lessee will be effective to destroy the squatter's title: *Fairweather* v *St Marylebone Property Co Ltd* [1963] AC 510. If in registered land, however, a lessee loses his lease by adverse possession and the squatter is registered with possessory title then a surrender by the original lessee will not be effective to destroy the squatter's title: *Spectrum Investment Co* v *Holmes* [1981] 1 All ER 6. In *Central London Commercial Estates Ltd* v *Kato Kagaku Ltd* [1998] 4 All ER 948 the matter was taken further. There a lease was originally granted for 94 years. A squatter had been in possession for over 12 years in circumstances which were effective to extinguish the lessee's rights, but the squatter had not applied to be registered with a possessory title. The original lessee then purported to surrender the lease. It was held that the surrender was ineffective; at the moment the lessee's rights were extinguished the lessee became a trustee and the squatter's rights were an overriding interest under s70(1) LRA. When the lease was surrendered it merged in the freehold title, but the trusteeship of the lease which had been established in relation to the squatter's title passed to the freeholder.

Qualified title

This is extremely rare. It may be granted by the Land Registry when on an application for absolute freehold or leasehold or good leasehold there is a defect, and it may be granted in relation to absolute freehold or leasehold or good leasehold.

Section 7 LRA states the effect of registration with qualified freehold title. Such registration has the same effect as registration with absolute title but there is excluded from the effect of registration such matter or matters as may be specified. Section 12 LRA contains similar provisions in relation to leaseholds.

Conversion of titles

Section 77 LRA contains provisions for conversion of titles:

1. Where land is registered with good leasehold title the registrar may, or if the proprietor applies and he is satisfied as to the superior title(s) must, upgrade the title to absolute.
2. If land is registered with possessory title the registrar may, or if the proprietor applies must if he is satisfied as to the title or the land has been registered for 12 years and the proprietor is in possession, convert the title to absolute freehold or good leasehold as the case may be.
3. If land is registered with qualified title it can be upgraded to absolute or good leasehold if the registrar is satisfied that the defect which gave rise to the registration with qualified title has been removed.

2.4 The register

Each registered estate is registered with its own title number. As each estate has its own title number there may, if there are for example a fee simple and a lease or leases, be more than one title and title number relating to the same piece of land.

The register is divided into three parts: see example in Appendix 1.

The property register contains details of the land. It may also contain details of any rights such as easements which benefit the land but this is not necessary.

The proprietorship register states the nature of the title, and gives the names and addresses of the proprietor or proprietors. It is in this register that cautions, inhibitions and restrictions are registered.

The charges register contains charges and incumbrances which adversely affect the land. This will contain details of any mortgages affecting the land. Under s26 LRA a charge is completed when details are entered on the register. All charges and mortgages have to be registered in registered land; there is no such thing as a first legal mortgage protected by deposit of deeds and exempt from registration. Other matters which can be registered include restrictive covenants and estate contracts. It is in the charges register that matters are protected by the registration of a notice.

Once land is registered the title deeds cease to be of relevance. What is determinative is the state of the register at the Land Registry. As there are no longer deeds, alternative provision is made in that once title is registered if there is no charge on the property the proprietor will be sent a land certificate. This is a copy of the register entries on the date specified contained in a formal cover and replaces the deeds. If a dealing with the land is to be registered, the land certificate must be produced to the Land Registry. If there is a charge, then no land certificate is issued but a charge certificate will be issued to the mortgagee. This is also a copy of the entries on the day the certificate is issued. If there more than one charge, then each mortgagee will be entitled to his own charge certificate. It must be emphasised that the charge or land certificate is of limited value in establishing the state of the title. It is what is registered at the Registry which is conclusive and a certificate is only evidence of the state of the register on the day on which it was prepared. It may therefore be out of date. If up-to-date copies of the register are required, then office copy entries may be requested which are copies of the register on a particular day and are as admissible in evidence to the same extent as the originals: s113 LRA. The Land Registry has recently stopped issuing charge certificates in some circumstances, the mortgagee's title consisting of office copy entries and the registration of the charge.

2.5 Third party rights

In registered land the distinction is between overriding and minor interests rather than legal and equitable interests which is the principle distinction in unregistered land. Overriding interests are those which are binding on registered land without being registered, although by virtue of s70(2) and (3) LRA they should, where appropriate, be noted on the register. Minor interests are those which need to be protected by an entry on the register.

Overriding interests

These are set out in s70(1) LRA which provides an exhaustive list of those matters which can have the status of overriding interests:

'a) rights of common, drainage rights, customary rights (until extinguished), public rights, profits à prendre, rights of sheepwalk, rights of way, watercourses, rights of water, and other easements not being equitable easements required to be protected by notice on the register;

b) liability to repair highways by reason of tenure, quit-rents, crown rents, heriots and other rents and charges (until extinguished) having their origin in tenure;

c) liability to repair the chancel of a church;

d) liability in respect of embankments and sea and river walls;

e) payments in lieu of tithe, and charges or annuities payable for the redemption of tithe rentcharges;

f) subject to the provisions of this Act, rights acquired or in course of being acquired under the Limitation Acts;

g) the rights of every person in actual occupation of the land or in receipt of the rents and profits thereof, save where inquiry is made of such person and the rights are not disclosed;

h) in the case of a possessory, qualified or good leasehold title, all estates, rights, interests, and powers excepted from the effect of registration;

i) rights under local land charges unless and until registered or protected on the register in the prescribed manner;

j) rights of fishing and sporting, seignorial and manorial rights of all descriptions (until extinguished), and franchises;

k) leases granted for a term not exceeding twenty-one years;

l) in respect of land registered before the commencement of the Act, rights to mines and minerals ...'

Some of these are obscure in the extreme, and are unlikely to be encountered; indeed the Law Commission has recommended the reduction in the number of overriding interests. The existence of overriding interests is the area where the LRA does not achieve its objective of defining the rights relating to land by reference to the register, since these matters affect the land without appearing on the register.

The following is an examination of those which are of most practical significance.

Section 70(1)(a)

This is a collection of various sorts of rights which can affect land. Some, such as rights of water or way, are merely examples of another category – easements. These are basically those rights which in unregistered land would have the status of legal rights in rem. However, in *Celsteel Ltd* v *Alton House Holdings Ltd* [1985] 2 All ER 562 it was held that by virtue of r258 LRR equitable easements can also have the status of overriding interests.

Section 70(1)(f)

It has been mentioned above that the effect of s75 LRA is that the proprietor holds the land on trust for a person who has acquired a title by adverse possession. Under this provision rights which have been acquired and which are being acquired under the Limitation Acts have the status of overriding interests. An example of the operation of this section can be seen in the case of *Bridges* v *Mees* [1957] Ch 475. In 1936 S orally agreed to purchase a piece of registered land from V Co for £7. He paid a deposit of £2, went into occupation and the following year paid the balance of the purchase money. There was no transfer, nor was any entry made on the register in relation to this transaction. In 1957 V Co went into liquidation. The Land Registry entries obviously still showed V Co as the proprietor of the piece of land occupied by S. The liquidator then sold the piece of land bought by S together with other land to P who was registered as proprietor with absolute title. It was held that S had acquired a title by adverse possession as he had been in occupation for over 12 years. The effect was that at the end of the 12-year period V Co's title was extinguished and V Co became a trustee for S who had an overriding interest. When P acquired the land he acquired it subject to any overriding interests, which included the rights which S had acquired. S was entitled to rectification and could be registered as proprietor of the piece of land he occupied. (If the sale to P had taken place in 1945, V Co's title would not have been extinguished as 12 years would not by then have elapsed. However, s70(1)(f) extends to rights which are in the course of being acquired and P in those circumstances would have acquired the land subject to the rights which S was in the process of acquiring. S would have acquired a title by adverse possession when the limitation period expired beginning with the date when he went into occupation; the sale to P in those circumstances would not have started time running again.)

Section 70(1)(g)

The rights of a person in actual occupation are an overriding interest. It must be emphasised that occupation itself is not a right; what this subsection protects is a proprietary right coupled with occupation. Equally, it need not be a right which is related to the fact of occupation, although it usually will be. For example, in *Webb* v *Pollmount Ltd* [1966] Ch 584 a tenant was in occupation under a lease. The lease included an option for him to purchase the freehold. This had the status of a minor interest and should have been protected by an entry on the register of the landlord's title but was not. The landlord sold the freehold reversion and the question was whether the tenant could exercise the option against the purchaser. It was held that he could as the option had the status of an overriding interest.

In *Williams and Glyn's Bank Ltd* v *Boland* [1981] AC 487 it was held that the interest of a wife who was an equitable tenant in common was within the section. In that case the husband was registered as sole proprietor, and by virtue of a financial contribution the wife had acquired an equitable interest. The husband mortgaged the property to the bank without the wife's involvement. It was held that she had an equitable interest which was an overriding interest and therefore was binding on the bank.

Under s70(1)(g) the person claiming the interest must be in occupation. A person may be in occupation even if temporarily absent, provided that he or she retains sufficient presence at the property. Whether a person is in occupation is a question of fact to be determined by reference to all the circumstances. In *Abbey National Building Society* v *Cann* [1991] AC 56 the House of Lords confirmed that the date for determining whether someone is in occupation for this provision is the date of completion of the transaction and not the date when the transaction is registered. The effect of these decisions is that a beneficiary under a trust who is in occupation when a transaction is completed has an overriding interest which will be binding on a purchaser. This is however subject to the general conveyancing provisions relating to overreaching of such interests. In *City of London Building Society* v *Flegg* [1988] AC 54 the House of Lords had to resolve the conflict between overriding interests and overreaching. In this case a husband and wife were registered joint proprietors. They and the wife's parents were equitable tenants in common as the parents had made a substantial financial contribution. The husband and wife charged the property without the parents' involvement. In possession proceedings taken by the mortgagee following default the parents claimed that they had an overriding interest which was binding on the mortgagee. The House of Lords held that in this situation the principles of overreaching applied; as this was a mortgage by two trustees, that was sufficient to overreach any equitable interest belonging to the parents which was transferred to the equity of redemption. The effect of this decision is to make it clear that where there are two trustees provided that the rights are capable of being overreached they will be. Of course, two trustees would not have made any difference in *Webb* v *Pollmount* as the option was not the sort of equitable interest which was capable of being overreached.

A spouse who has no proprietary interest in the property cannot have an overriding interest under this provision, but can protect his or her statutory right of occupation by registering a notice under the Family Law Act 1996; such a statutory right does not have the status of an overriding interest.

Section 70(1)(i)

Under the Local Land Charges Act 1975 local authorities have to keep registers of various matters. These do not normally appear on the land register. They are given the status of overriding interests which means that they are binding on the land even though not protected at the Land Registry. The conveyancing implication is that local searches have to be carried when the land is registered: see Chapter 5.

Section 70(1)(k)

This applies to leases granted and does not therefore include agreements for leases which have not been granted, as the use of the word grant implies the creation of a legal estate (which can of course be oral or in writing if less than three years: s54(2) LPA). However, although an agreement for a lease will not be an overriding interest, the interest of a tenant under an agreement for a lease would be an overriding interest under s70(1)(g) if, as would be normal, the tenant is in actual occupation.

Minor interests

These are defined in s3(xv) LRA as:

> '... interests not capable of being disposed of or created by registered dispositions and capable of being overridden (whether or not a purchaser has notice thereof) by the proprietors unless protected as provided by this Act, and all rights and interests which are not registered or protected on the register and are not overriding interests ...'

There are various sorts of minor interests. First, there are interests under trusts. These will be overreached provided the relevant legal formalities are complied with. Second, there are dispositions of registered land between completion and registration. As in registered land legal title only passes on registration, the interest of a purchaser will rank as a minor interest until registration, unless of course he is in occupation in which case he will have an overriding interest under s70(1)(g). Third, there are equitable interests which need to be protected by an entry on the register and which broadly correspond to those matters which can be registered under the LCA in unregistered land.

There are various methods of protecting minor interests; it should be noted that in some cases an unregistered minor interest may take effect as an overriding interest under s70(1)(g) above.

Notice

This is entered in the charges register of the title affected. It gives details of the interest protected. In order to register a notice the land certificate must be produced to the Land Registry and therefore registration of a notice generally requires the co-operation of the proprietor. However, when the land is subject to a registered charge no land certificate will have been issued and will be retained by the registry and therefore a notice can be registered. Also, the certificate does not have to be produced when a Family Law Act notice is registered to protect a spouse's statutory right of occupation. A notice is a means of protecting a right or interest which is otherwise valid under general land law principles; it does not make valid something which is otherwise invalid. For example, a notice relating to a positive covenant will not make the burden pass, as only the burden of negative covenants passes under the rule in *Tulk* v *Moxhay*, and notice of an option which has lapsed will not make the option exercisable.

Caution

Any person interested in registered land may protect that interest by the registration of a caution in the proprietorship register. Many interests can be so protected – eg estate contracts, charging orders, interests under trusts of land. The registered caution does not specify the nature of the interest protected but merely states the fact that there is a caution, the date it was registered and in whose favour it is made. A caution does not effect substantive registration of the matter protected, nor does it confer any priority, but it gives the cautioner the right to be given notice of any application to register a dealing thereby affording him the opportunity to object. If he does not object after the prescribed time – normally 14 days – the registration can proceed. If he does object then the Registrar determines how the matter is to proceed by, for example, cancelling the caution, refusing the registration or permitting registration subject to the protected interest. In practice, matters rarely get to this stage as a purchaser who discovers a caution will require the matter to be resolved before proceeding to completion. As a sanction to prevent the use of cautions without just cause, under s56(4) LRA a person who lodges a caution without reasonable cause is liable to compensate any person who suffers loss as the result of the caution.

Inhibition
The court or the Registrar may register an inhibition; a person cannot register an inhibition himself but has to apply for it to be registered. It has the effect of preventing the registration of any dealing with the registered land, either generally or for a fixed period. The commonest inhibition is a bankruptcy inhibition registered on the bankruptcy of the proprietor. Other examples could be, for example, when the deeds have been lost or stolen in order to prevent fraud. An inhibition is registered in the proprietorship register.

Restriction
This is also registered in the proprietorship register. It is, as the name suggests, a restriction on the ability of the proprietor to deal with the registered land. It will normally set out procedures which have to be followed and gives information as to what steps need to be taken. For example, where there is a trust of land two trustees are needed to overreach equitable interests. A restriction will make it clear that two trustees can sell but one cannot. Similarly, if land is owned by trustees and they can only deal with it with the consent of a specified person or, in the case of a charity, the Charity Commissioners, then the restriction will state that no disposition is to be registered unless the relevant consent has been given. In essence, a restriction sets out requirements with which a purchaser has to comply if he wants a good title.

2.6 Effect of transfers

Under s20(1) LRA, a disposition of a registered freehold absolute title or the grant of a lease out of it for valuable consideration operates when the disposition or grant is registered to confer on the transferee the fee simple or term of years subject to incumbrances and other entries appearing on the register and overriding interests but free of all other estates and interests. In unregistered land, under the LCA a purchaser takes free of a registrable but unregistered land charge even if he has actual notice of it. There is a similar provision in registered land in s59(6) LRA, namely a purchaser acquiring title under a registered disposition is not concerned with any matter which should have been protected by an entry on the register and which is not so protected whether or not he has express implied or constructive notice of that matter. A purchaser in this context means a purchaser in good faith for valuable consideration and includes a mortgagee, lessee or any other person who acquires any interest in the land for valuable consideration (which includes marriage but not a nominal consideration). This definition is different from that in the LCA where no requirement of good faith is needed: *Midland Bank Trust Co Ltd* v *Green* [1981] AC 513 (see Chapter 11, section 11.2). If the disposition is made without valuable consideration, then the transferee or grantee will be subject to minor interests subject to which the transferor or grantor held the land whether or not they are protected by registration: s20(4) LRA.

2.7 Rectification and indemnity

Rectification

It has been emphasised that in registered land the state of the register is conclusive. That is the case even if the register is wrong. If the register is wrong then it can only be corrected – or rectified – on the grounds, and following the procedure, set out in the LRA. The grounds on which the register can be rectified include cases where there are mistakes on the register, where matters have been registered which should not have been and where matters which should have been registered have been omitted.

Section 82(1) LRA sets out the procedure as follows.

The register may be rectified pursuant to an order of the court or of the registrar (in the latter case however subject to a right of appeal to the court) in the following circumstances:

1. if a court has decided that a person is entitled to an estate right or interest in or to registered land and in consequence the court decides the register needs to be rectified and makes an order to that effect;
2. if the court on the application of any person aggrieved by an entry in or omission from the register makes an order for rectification;
3. at any time with the consent of all persons interested;
4. where an entry has been obtained by fraud;
5. where two or more persons are by mistake registered as proprietors of the same estate or charge;
6. where a mortgagee has by mistake been registered as proprietor of the land;
7. where a legal estate has been registered in the name of a person who if the land were not registered would not be the estate owner;
8. in any other case where by reason of error or omission or because of an entry made under a mistake, it may be deemed just to rectify the register.

There is an important limitation on the power of rectification in s82(3). This subsection proves that except for the purpose of giving effect to an overriding interest (which is merely making the register reflect what the actual position is) or an order of the court, the register cannot be rectified so as to affect the title of a proprietor who is in possession, unless the proprietor has caused or substantially contributed to the error or omission by fraud or lack of proper care, or unless it would be unjust not to rectify the register against him.

Indemnity

One of the principles underlying registration is that the register should be conclusive and that the accuracy of the register is guaranteed by the state. The corollary of this is that if there is a mistake in the register then there is, in some circumstances, a right to compensation – or an indemnity as it is described. The provisions as to indemnity are contained in s83 LRA; a new s83 was inserted by the LRA 1997.

Under s83(1), where the register is rectified, a person suffering loss because of the rectification is entitled to be indemnified. Also, if the register is rectified any person in whose favour it is rectified who has suffered loss as the result of the error or omission which has been rectified is entitled to an indemnity. Under s83(2) where an error or omission is not rectified, any person suffering loss as the result of the error or omission is entitled to an indemnity. (There was a significant alteration in 1997. Under the original s83 there was an entitlement to an indemnity if the register was rectified or if it was not. There was no entitlement to an indemnity if the register was rectified and there was still loss. That has now been changed.)

There is also a right to an indemnity if a person suffers loss because of loss or damage to a document lodged at the Land Registry or because of an error in an official search: s83(3).

Under s83(4), subject to subsequent provisions of the section, a proprietor of land claiming in good faith under a forged disposition is, where the register is rectified, deemed to have suffered loss because of the rectification and is entitled to be indemnified.

Section 83(5) states that an indemnity is not payable: '(a) on account of any loss suffered by a claimant wholly or partly as a result of his own fraud or wholly as the result of his lack of proper care'. Under s83(6) where the loss is due partly to his lack of care any indemnity payable is to be reduced by such amount as is fair, having regard to his share in responsibility for the loss. (This was another change effected in 1997. Prior to that date if the claimant contributed to the loss through lack of care he lost his right to an indemnity entirely; now responsibility and compensation can be apportioned.)

If an indemnity is paid in respect of the loss of an estate, interest or charge, under s83(8) the amount paid shall not exceed:

'a) where the register is not rectified, the value of the estate, interest or charge at the time when the error ... which caused the loss was made;

(b) where the register is rectified, the value (if there had been no rectification) of the estate, interest or charge, immediately before the time of rectification.'

The indemnity can also include reasonable costs and expenses.

If an indemnity is paid the registrar can take steps to recover it from any person who caused or substantially contributed to the loss by fraud. Also, the registrar can enforce any right which the claimant could have enforced if the indemnity had not been paid, and if the register is rectified the registrar can pursue any action which the person in whose favour the register has been rectified could have pursued in the absence of rectification: s83(10).

3

The Contract – Formalities

3.1 Introduction

3.2 Formalities

3.3 Constructive trusts and estoppel

3.4 Conditional contracts

3.1 Introduction

The first stage in a conveyancing transaction is that the seller prepares the contract. This is the crucial part of the whole transaction since it defines the parties' obligations which have to be performed at completion.

As in many legal transactions the first draft of the contract is the basis on which negotiations take place. It can be amended and altered until it is agreed by both parties. In preparing the contract the seller's solicitor will have the deeds, his client's instructions, estate agents' particulars, etc, and the task is to collate all this information and produce a coherent document.

The seller as part of the conveyancing transaction has to deduce title, ie prove that the seller is legally entitled and able to sell. The seller should check the title at the outset so that if there are any problems they can be resolved. Also, it is normal, whether or not the Conveyancing Protocol is being used, for evidence of the seller's title to be supplied to the buyer with the draft contract so the seller has to prepare this evidence in any event.

3.2 Formalities

Section 2 Law of Property (Miscellaneous Provisions) Act 1989

Section 2 of the Law of Property (Miscellaneous Provisions) Act (LP(MP)A) 1989 sets out the legal requirements for contracts entered into on and after 27 September 1989 and replaced s40 LPA. It does not apply to contracts to grant a lease for three years or less, contracts made at public auctions and contracts regulated under the

Financial Services Act 1986, and does not affect the creation or operation of resulting implied or constructive trusts: s2(5). The section provides:

> '(1) A contract for the sale or other disposition of an interest in land can only be made in writing and only by incorporating all the terms which the parties have expressly agreed in one document or, where contracts are exchanged, in each.
> (2) The terms may be incorporated in a document either by being set out in it or by reference to some other document.
> (3) The document incorporating the terms or, where contracts are exchanged, one of the documents incorporating them (but not necessarily the same one) must be signed by or on behalf of each party to the contract.'

Under s2 the contract must be made in writing. This is a formal requirement and failure to observe it prevents a contract coming into existence. By contrast, under s40 LPA, the contract, to be enforceable, had to be evidenced in writing, ie there could be a valid oral contract made in accordance with normal contractual principles, but to be enforceable there had to be signed written evidence. Under s2 absence of writing does not make the contract valid but unenforceable, but void. As any written evidence could satisfy s40, correspondence prior to exchange of contracts was headed 'subject to contract'. This formula denied the existence of a contract and meant that such correspondence could not be treated as written evidence of an oral contract. As s2 prevents a contract coming into existence the use of the term 'subject to contract' is no longer necessary.

The requirement is that the contract must contain all the terms, and it would therefore seem that the omission of a relevant provision could prevent a contract coming into existence. The courts have in some cases managed to avoid the drastic consequences of this. For example, the courts have construed a clause as a collateral contract, as in *Tootal Clothing Ltd* v *Guinea Properties Management Ltd* (1992) 64 P & CR 452 where there was a contract for the grant of a lease. A provision confirming that the landlord would contribute to the costs of works to be done by the tenant was omitted. The lease was granted, the tenant did the work but the landlord declined to pay, alleging the agreement was void because it failed to comply with s2. The court held that s2 did not apply to executed contracts where the parties had performed their obligations, as here, but only to executory contracts. Also, the court held that the agreement as to the contribution was a collateral contract which could be severed from the main contract and thereby escape the requirements s2. If a provision is relatively minor and does not go to the heart of the transaction the court may be prepared to sever the offending clause rather than invalidate the whole transaction. Also, if a clause has been omitted it may be possible to apply for rectification on the basis that the contract as drawn does not accurately reflect the common intention of the parties.

The contract must be signed by all parties. It appears that signed now means signed. In *Firstpost Homes Ltd* v *Johnson* [1995] 4 All ER 355 the Court of Appeal had to consider this. P through their director, G, reached an oral agreement for the purchase of land from S. G typed a letter for S to sign containing S's address and the name and address of G as purchaser and referring to the land 'shown on the enclosed plan'. S signed the letter and the accompanying plan and G signed the plan only and not the letter. S died and the plaintiffs applied for specific performance. The Court of Appeal held that the two documents were separate and could not be construed as one document as G had not signed the letter. Each party had to sign, and the inclusion of G's typed name and address in the letter did not amount to signature, which meant for the purposes of s2 signature with one's own hand. The Court said that the purpose of the Act was to achieve certainty, and to ensure that the terms of a contract could be ascertained by referring to one document only rather than by constructing a contract from a variety of documents.

It will be noted that s2 applies not only to land but also an interest in land. Prior to 1989 a common form of charge was to deposit the deeds or land certificate with a lender as security The deposit was considered part performance of a contract to create a legal mortgage which took effect as an equitable charge. This form of charge was no longer possible after 1989. In *United Bank of Kuwait plc* v *Sahib* [1996] 3 All ER 215 the Court of Appeal held that s2 was designed to create certainty. Part performance had been abolished and deposit of deeds would no longer be sufficient to create an equitable charge as there could not be part performance of a contract which did not exist.

Variations

It should be noted that s2 LP(MP)A 1989 not only applies to the making of contracts but also to any subsequent variation. In *McCausland* v *Duncan Lawrie Ltd* [1997] 1 WLR 38 there was a contract for the sale of land. The completion date was arranged for a Sunday and the parties' solicitors agreed to change completion date to the previous Friday. The buyer failed to complete on the varied date and the seller subsequently rescinded the contract. The court held that the variation was invalid, the contract as originally drawn still obtained and the rescission was invalid. However, a limitation on this can be seen in the case of *Target Holdings Ltd* v *Priestley* [1999] Lloyd's Rep Bank 175. There, a husband and wife were joint owners of a house. In 1989 T advanced a substantial sum to finance the husband's business to be secured by a mortgage. One of the clauses in the mortgage stated that the mortgagors' personal liability to repay did not arise unless and until the proceeds of a sale by T were insufficient to repay sums due. Arrears mounted and a manager of T and the borrowers agreed that the liability would be discharged if they repaid the capital sum by instalments over 14 years, they accepted immediate personal liability and the total sum outstanding would become due in the event of default in payment of the monthly instalments. T subsequently claimed that arrears under the original mortgage were accumulating. The court held first that there was consideration furnished to T as the borrowers had accepted an immediate personal liability in place of the conditional liability under the original mortgage. The court also considered the effect of s2. The court stated that there was a distinction between contracts for the sale or disposition of an interest in land and contracts arising out of such a disposition. Section 2 applied to the former but not the latter. As the mortgage fell into this latter category s2 did not apply.

Options

There was initially some concern as to how s2 LP(MP)A 1989 applied to options. The main question was whether s2 applied to the notice exercising an option, ie whether it had to be signed by both parties. In *Spiro* v *Glencrown Properties* [1991] Ch 537 the court had to consider this. Contracts were exchanged, correctly signed, which granted to X an option to purchase land. X sent a letter exercising the option and then failed to complete. He subsequently contended that the exercise of the option was invalid as it did not comply with s2 as it was not signed by the other party. There had in earlier cases been discussions as to the precise legal nature of an option – for example, was it an irrevocable offer or a conditional contract. It was held in *Spiro* that an option was sui juris. The exercise of the option did not have to comply with s2; the option was validly exercised when the letter was sent as specified in the contract. It was emphasised, however, that the contract granting the option must comply with s2 but, as long as it does so, the exercise of the option does not.

3.3 Constructive trusts and estoppel

In order to mitigate the rigours of s40 LPA, equity developed the doctrine of part performance. In essence, if there was a valid but unenforceable contract for the sale of land which one party had performed, the other party could not use the absence of formalities to defend unconscionable conduct. This doctrine was one example of the wider principle that equity would not allow a statute to be used as an instrument of fraud. However, with the repeal of s40, part performance disappeared.

There were, however, other equitable remedies available in a conveyancing context. The principle of proprietary estoppel could operate. If one party creates an expectation upon which the other party relies, in some circumstances it would be inequitable to allow the first party to go back on his word. In *Inwards* v *Baker* [1965] 2 QB 29 a father allowed his son to build a bungalow on his land. In the father's will the land was left to someone else. It was held that there was an estoppel and the son could not be removed. In *ER Ives Investment Ltd* v *High* [1967] 2 QB 379 X erected a building on a piece of land. The foundations encroached onto Y's land. They agreed that the foundations could remain and that Y could have a right of way over X's land. Y subsequently built a garage on his land which could only be accessed over the right of way and he also contributed to the upkeep of the right of way. The agreement for the right of way (not in a deed) was not registered. X sold his land to the plaintiff, subject to Y's rights, and the plaintiff tried to stop Y using the track, alleging that this right was not binding because of the absence of registration. It was held that he could not. The court emphasised the mutuality in the original agreement, and referred to *Halsall* v *Brizell* [1957] Ch 169, where purchasers of houses who used a road had to accept the obligation to maintain that went with it. Also, the court referred to X's acquiescence and the fact that as the plaintiffs had bought with notice of Y's rights, they were bound by it.

An alternative remedy was that provided by the use of the constructive trust which can be seen in *Bannister* v *Bannister* [1948] 2 All ER 133. Here the defendant owned two houses and sold them to her brother-in-law, the plaintiff, at a price well below market value, under an oral agreement whereby the brother-in-law agreed that she could stay in one of the houses for as long as she wanted. The brother-in-law in due course claimed possession. The court held that the plaintiff held the house upon trust to allow the defendant to live there for as long as she wanted. Another example can be seen in *Binions* v *Evans* [1972] Ch 359 where trustees entered into an agreement with the defendant, the widow of an employee, to allow her to stay in a cottage for as long as she wanted as tenant at will provided that she kept it in good order and did not part with possession. The cottage was sold to the plaintiff expressly subject to her tenancy. The court held that the plaintiff held the property upon a constructive trust to allow her to stay in the cottage.

The case of *Yaxley* v *Gotts & Gotts* [1999] 3 WLR 1217 has made it clear that the availability of these remedies has survived the repeal of s40 and the introduction of s2, and that oral agreements may still in some circumstances be enforceable. In this case the second defendant made an oral agreement with the plaintiff whereby he would give the plaintiff the ground floor of a house he was going to buy in exchange for the plaintiff's labour and materials in converting the property and thereafter managing the lettings. The house was purchased in the name of the first defendant, the second defendant's son. The plaintiff carried out his part of the agreement but the defendants then refused to give him any interest in the property. It was accepted that part performance had not survived the repeal of s40 and could not therefore assist the plaintiff. He claimed an estoppel, but the defendant argued that the principle of estoppel could not make valid a transaction which Parliament had, as a matter of policy, made invalid. The court held that the situations in which estoppel could arise were so varied that it would not be correct to say that estoppel could not apply. It was also pointed out that at a very general level there was considerable similarity between part performance, proprietary estoppel and constructive trusts, as they were all concerned to give relief against unconscionable conduct. The agreement was void as it did not comply with s2 and part performance could not apply. The trial judge had held that there was an oral agreement which had been adopted by the defendants and the plaintiff was entitled to ownership of the ground floor by virtue of proprietary estoppel. The Court of Appeal confirmed that decision, and also held that the facts as found would equally have justified the finding that the plaintiff was entitled to an interest under a constructive trust.

3.4 Conditional contracts

For a contract to exist there must be an unconditional offer and acceptance. The parties may agree to a sale of property but the agreement may be stated to be 'subject to ...', ie subject to a certain matter. The effect of this qualification varies. It is a question of interpretation in each particular case as to the effect of the condition.

Condition which prevents a contract coming into existence

If a condition has this effect, the condition as expressed prevents a binding contract coming into existence. The use of the words 'subject to contract' normally have this effect as they expressly deny the existence of a contract, although the courts may ignore these words if they are meaningless. In *Alpenstow Ltd* v *Regalian Properties plc* [1985] 2 All ER 545 a professionally drafted agreement was stated to be subject to contract which, if interpreted to deny the existence of a contract, would have had the effect of rendering the agreement of no effect. The court held that the clear meaning of the words would not be applied as in the context of the transaction they did not make sense.

Condition precedent to performance

In many cases the imposition of a condition may result in a concluded contract, but performance is subject to the fulfilment of the condition. In cases such as these the condition is a term of the contract. The contract is binding subject to the terms of the condition and subject to interpretation of the terms, only non-fulfilment will enable a party to withdraw or discharge the contract without the other party's agreement. Examples of such a condition are:

1. subject to the purchaser arranging a satisfactory mortgage;
2. subject to planning permission;
3. subject to satisfactory searches;
4. subject to a satisfactory survey;
5. subject to the landlord giving consent (in the case of an assignment of a lease or grant of a sub-lease).

The condition must be precise and certain; if it is not the agreement will be void. Certainty is needed because it has to be determined whether or not the condition has been satisfied, as if it has the contract becomes unconditional and has to be performed. The courts will try to give a condition a reasonable interpretation and thereby escape the consequence of holding the agreement of no effect. In *Lee Parker* v *Izzett (No 2)* [1972] 2 All ER 800 there was a contract 'subject to the purchaser obtaining a satisfactory mortgage'. It was held that that was too vague to be valid, as the condition did not specify anything – not only matters such as interest rate but also the essentials of amount and terms of repayment. In *Janmohamed* v *Hassam* (1976) 241 EG 609, however, a condition that the purchaser was to obtain a mortgage 'satisfactory to him' was upheld. The court implied a term that satisfaction was not reasonably to be refused, and therefore the term was not so vague as to render the agreement void. It would seem that where a condition states that a contract is subject to a satisfactory mortgage or satisfactory replies to searches, the courts will be ready to uphold the condition by implying a requirement of reasonableness – ie that the mortgage or replies must be such as would satisfy a reasonable purchaser.

In order to avoid problems the condition should be precisely defined, so that the events on which the contract becomes unconditional are clearly understandable.

It will normally be desirable to specify a time limit. If such is specified then it must be strictly observed. If no time limit is specified then the condition must be satisfied within a reasonable time. If the condition is not satisfied then the contract cannot be enforced. There is however a limitation on this in that if the condition depends on a party acting then he must do so. Thus, if there is a contract conditional on a satisfactory survey, it is implied that the purchaser will commission a survey, consider the report and then make a bona fide decision in the light of the contents: *Ee* v *Kakar* (1970) 40 P & CR 223. If he fails to commission a survey, then he will not be able to rely on the non-fulfilment. Similarly, if a contract is dependent on a mortgage offer, the purchaser would have to apply for a mortgage advance.

In *Millers Wharf Partnership Ltd* v *Corinthian Column Ltd* [1991] 1 EGLR 192 the effect of time limits was considered. There, a contract was conditional upon the seller obtaining all necessary consents and approvals by a certain date, in default of which at any time thereafter either party could serve a notice on the other rescinding the agreement. The permissions were not obtained by the due date but were obtained later. The purchaser then served a notice rescinding the agreement. It was held that he was entitled to rescind the agreement and to have his deposit returned. The wording was quite clear, and the right to rescind arose on the date when the permission had not been obtained. The fact that the permissions were obtained by the time of the notice to rescind was not the issue. The purchaser had obtained a vested right, which he could exercise unless he could be taken to have waived it or acquiesced in the default which on the facts he had not.

Waiver

The issue of whether a condition can be waived was addressed in *Heron Garage Properties Ltd* v *Moss* [1974] 1 All ER 421. In this case there was a contract which was conditional upon planning permission being obtained, and the condition affected other matters such as completion date. There was also a provision that if planning permission could not be obtained then either party could determine the contract. The purchaser wished to waive the condition and purchase without permission being obtained. The court held that a purchaser could only waive a condition if it was for his exclusive benefit and this had to be clear either on the face of the contract or by necessary implication. It would not be appropriate to go outside the contract to see where the benefit lay. The purchaser here could not waive the condition as it was not for his exclusive benefit, as failure to obtain planning permission gave the other party a right to determine the agreement, and the clause defining the condition affected other provisions in the agreement which could not be severed.

4

The Contract – Contents

4.1 Introduction

4.2 The contract

4.3 Special conditions

4.4 Void conditions

4.1 Introduction

Although it is not necessary to have a contract for the sale of land, in most cases there will be one. Nowadays the contract will probably be prepared on a standard form and it will usually incorporate a set of standard conditions. The Standard Conditions of Sale 3rd edition 1995 are now the ones which are used and to which reference will be made. They are reproduced in full in Appendix 6. As has been mentioned in Chapter 1 (section 1.1), if the contract prepared by the parties does not make express provision for a matter, then the open contract rules will apply. Where appropriate, the difference between the Standard Conditions and the open contract rules will be examined.

A typical contract is set out in Appendix 2 and will be examined.

It should be noted that in a normal conveyancing transaction the contract sets out the obligations which will be carried out on completion. The contract does not transfer the legal estate, does not impose covenants and does not create easements. It does however state that the transaction defined in the contract will be carried out by the purchase deed. It is that document which will (subject to registration) transfer the legal estate, will impose covenants and will grant or reserve easements, etc. The transaction as defined by the contract, nothing more and nothing less, is carried out on completion and by the transfer deed. It is therefore vital that the contract is accurate and contains all necessary provisions as, subject to rectification, it will be too late after exchange of contracts to add to, take away or modify the terms of the contract. Also, a failure by either party to perform the obligations as set out in the contract will result in a breach of contract.

4.2 The contract

The following is a commentary on the Law Society's form of contract (see Appendix 2) which is commonly used in conveyancing transactions and an examination of the relevant clauses in the Standard Conditions.

1. *The heading.* This makes it plain that the Standard Conditions of Sale are incorporated. It is open to the parties to exclude or modify any particular condition in their own special conditions but, if this form is used, then the Standard Conditions will apply unless they are specifically modified or excluded.
2. *The agreement date.* This is left blank when the contract is drafted. This date will be inserted on exchange, as it is the date on which the contract comes into existence and the legal obligations of both parties are created.
3. The details of the *seller* and *buyer* are set out.
4. *The particulars.* This contains a legal and physical description of the property and it states whether the property is freehold or leasehold. It should be born in mind that under s60 LPA a conveyance of freehold land passes the fee simple without express words. There should be an accurate physical description of the property. In unregistered land, this description will frequently be that which was used in previous conveyances, but care should be taken to ensure that it is accurate. If part of land in a title is being sold then reference may well be made to a plan, and when part is being sold particular care is needed in defining the property. If there is a plan the relationship between the plan and the verbal description needs to be addressed. If the plan and verbal description coincide there is no problem, but difficulties arise if they do not. If there is a discrepancy, then which prevails? If the verbal description is in the following form, ie 'the land known as ... for the purpose of identification only shown edged red on the annexed plan', then the words have priority. If, however, the words used are in the form 'the land known as ... more particularly delineated on the plan annexed', then the plan will be regarded as determinative. The preparation of a plan may be a very important exercise. In *Scarfe* v *Adams* [1981] 1 All ER 843 the Court of Appeal was trenchant in its criticism of what it called 'sloppy conveyancing'. A coach house was being divided into two separate properties. The only plan was an extract from the 1:2500 Ordnance Survey map, described as for convenience only, its accuracy was not guaranteed and it was expressly excluded from the contract. There was a dispute as to the precise boundary between the two properties. The verbal description did not help and the small-scale plan was worse than useless. The dispute eventually had to be resolved by reference to auction particulars which referred to architect's drawings prepared in connection with the conversion.

It should be noted that in *Jackson* v *Bishop* (1979) 48 P & CR 57 the Court of Appeal held that developers of an estate owed a duty of care to the purchasers to prepare an accurate plan.

The basic principle in interpreting documents is that in the absence of ambiguity it is not permissible to refer to extrinsic evidence to vary or contradict a description which is clear. Only if it is not clear can reference be made: *Scarfe* v *Adams* above. In *Freeguard* v *Rogers* [1999] 1 WLR 1999 an option (not professionally prepared) was granted for the purchase of a 'freehold house and garage known as ...'. The house was registered with a freehold title, the garage with a separate leasehold title. The option referred to an incorrect title number which related to neither the house nor the garage. Both parties thought they were dealing with a freehold property but that was not conclusive. The use of words 'known as' made it inevitable that recourse would have to be had to extrinsic evidence as the description was not clear. The court referred to draft agent's particulars and the physical layout – an independent observer would have said that the property was a house and garage because, for example, there was a door from the garage to the garden. The court concluded that the description included the house and garage.

The seller is not obliged to define the boundaries with precision:

'SC 4.3.1 The seller need not:
a) prove the exact boundaries of the property
b) prove who owns fences, ditches, hedges or walls
c) separately identify parts of the property with different titles
further than he may be able to do from information in his possession.
4.3.2 The buyer may, if it is reasonable, require the seller to make or obtain, pay for and hand over a statutory declaration about facts relevant to the matters mentioned in condition 4.3.1. The form of the declaration is to be agreed by the buyer, who must not unreasonably withhold his agreement.'

In defining properties there are various presumptions and a recent case has shown how they can still apply and how the issues of boundary disputes can be tackled. In *Alan Wibberley Building Ltd* v *Insley* [1999] 2 All ER 897 the House of Lords confirmed that the hedge and ditch presumption still applied. This states that where two fields are divided by a hedge and ditch the boundary is normally the side of the ditch furthest from the hedge. In this case a conveyance described the property by reference to an Ordnance Survey map which defined the boundary between two fields as the middle of a hedge. Despite the clear wording used, the House of Lords held that the boundary was where the presumption would have put it. Evidence is needed to rebut the presumption and here the court concluded that there had in the past been a mistake in defining the property in the way it was described. If the presumption had been rebutted and did not apply, a previous landowner would have retained a useless strip of land between the middle of the hedge and the far side of the ditch which could not have been what was intended. In this case the court emphasised the general nature of boundaries, and the problems in being absolutely precise. (Indeed, r258 LRR states that in the context of registered land boundaries as defined on the plan are only general.)

5. *Root of title/ title number.* One of the obligations of the seller in a conveyancing transaction is to deduce title, ie produce evidence to show that he can sell and give the buyer a good title. (For detail on this see Chapter 8.) In registered land the evidence of title will be office copies of entries in the Land Registry, and here is specified the title number of the property. If the land is unregistered then the seller has to prove that he and his predecessors have owned the property for at least 15 years. He does this by producing evidence of the documents and events for that period. The title period will begin with a document at least 15 years old – the root of title – and that document is specified in the contract.

6. *Incumbrances on the property.* This issue is related to the seller's duty of disclosure: see Chapter 5, section 5.1. Incumbrances affecting the property have to be disclosed. The incumbrances which have to be specified here are those matters:

a) which are in existence; and
b) which will bind the property after the purchaser has acquired it.

Therefore, incumbrances not to be specified here are those matters which will come into existence on completion, eg new restrictive covenants to be imposed or easements which will be reserved. Provision for matters such as these which are not in existence at the date of contract, but which will be created on completion, must be made by means of an appropriate special condition. Also incumbrances not needing to specified here are those matters which are in existence at the date of the contract but which will not affect the property after the sale, such as a mortgage which will be discharged. A mortgage affects the title and has to be disclosed as a purchaser is entitled to see that appropriate arrangements can be made for its discharge, but it is not an incumbrance which needs to be specified. Only those incumbrances which will continue to bind the property after completion have to be set out here. The significance of this is in SC 3.1.1, which states that the seller is selling the property free from incumbrances, other than those mentioned in condition 3.1.2.

> 'SC 3.1.2 The encumbrances subject to which the property is sold are:
> a) those mentioned in the agreement
> b) those discoverable by inspection of the property before the contract
> c) those the seller does not and could not know about
> d) entries made before the date of the contract in any public register except those maintained by HM Land Registry or its Land Charges Department or by Companies House
> e) public requirements.

Matters contained in (b) to (e) do not have to be specified in the contract as incumbrances. Taking each in turn:

a) These are those matters specified in the contract and will include matters such as restrictive covenants even though registered, and also any overriding interests in registered land.

b) These are matters discoverable on inspection. It would be dangerous for a seller to rely on this, and it is far preferable for the seller to specify precisely those adverse rights which will continue to affect the property after completion.

c) These are self-explanatory.

d) It is important to note that matters entered in the Land Registry, Land Charges Registry and Companies Registry do not come under (d), and if therefore there is any matter which is registered in any of those registers which will continue to bind the property after completion (such as a restrictive covenant or equitable easement), this must be specifically mentioned in the contract so that it comes within (a) above. The most important matters under (d) are local land charges and commons and village green register entries. Searches in these registers must be made prior to contract as anything registered in them will affect the property. The contract states that the property is sold subject to them and so the seller will not be in breach in relation to a matter registered in those registers.

   (Reference may be made here to s24 of the Law of Property Act 1969. Under the land charges legislation the general rule is that registration is notice and if a charge is registered a purchaser has notice. Under s24, however, where there is a contract for the sale of land, registration of a land charge does not give a purchaser notice thereof at the time the contract was made; whether he had notice at that time is to be determined by reference to his actual knowledge. Hence a Land Charges Registry search is not normally done before exchange. This section does not apply to conveyances and so searches have to be done before completion.)

e) Public requirements are defined in SC 1.1.1(j) as 'any notice, order or proposal given or made (whether before or after the date of the contract) by a body acting on statutory authority.'

   Under SC 3.1.4 the buyer has to bear the cost of complying with any public requirement and has to indemnify the seller against any liability resulting from it.

   Under SC 3.1.3, after the contract is made the seller must inform the buyer without delay of any new public requirement and of anything which he learns about concerning any incumbrances subject to which the property is sold.

Under an open contract the seller has to disclose latent defects in title. Defects in title are those matters which affect the ownership of the property and his ability to deal with it. They include matters such as restrictive covenants, easements, mortgages, etc. Latent defects are those which would not be discoverable on reasonable inspection of the property, and as they are within the exclusive knowledge of the seller he is under an obligation to disclose them.

7. *Title guarantee.* The contract will specify the title guarantee to be given in the conveyance/transfer as full or limited. (See Chapter 10, section 10.3 for further discussion on this.) Covenants for title were originally included in a conveyance because of the operation of the contractual principle of merger, whereby where there was a contract which was performed by a conveyance, the contract merged in the conveyance and obligations created by the contract ceased to exist. To give a purchaser some protection after completion, covenants for title were inserted in the conveyance. The principle of merger applies unless there is a contrary provision, which there is in the Standard Conditions. Standard Condition 7.4 provides that 'Completion does not cancel liability to perform any outstanding obligation under this contract.'

8. *Completion date.* Under the open contract rules, completion is to take place a reasonable time after exchange which is obviously unsatisfactory, so the parties will agree on a completion date before contracts are exchanged. Under the Standard Conditions completion is 20 working days from exchange: SC 6.1.1. This is normally replaced by an express contractual provision in the contract specifying the completion date. The general principle is that when dealing with completion, time is not of the essence (SC 6.1.1) and therefore a failure by either party to complete on the due date does not enable the other party to treat the contract as discharged. It gives him remedies (see Chapter 12) but is does not terminate the contract automatically.

   A special condition can make completion date of the essence, which would have the effect of enabling a party not in default to terminate the contract if the completion date was not met. Such a clause is exceptional and would normally be rejected by the other party. An example of where such a clause might be inserted would be if a developer wished, for tax or financial reasons, to encourage completion before the end of the financial year, and offered special terms such as a reduced price. The sole purpose of the reduction would be to encourage completion; if completion did not take place then the rationale for the discount would go. In such a circumstance, the developer might consider making completion date of the essence, with the result that if the buyer does not complete on the due date, the developer is not obliged to sell at the reduced price.

9. *Contract rate.* This is the rate at which interest is calculated for delayed completion. It will be the Law Society's rate unless an alternative is specified.

10. *Purchase price.* This is the price for the land. It is the price to be included in the conveyance, and it is the price on which the stamp duty liability is calculated.

11. *Deposit.* There is no general principle in contract which states that a deposit has to be paid. If in any contract there is to be a deposit then an express term to that effect must be included. In SC 2.2 there is provision for a deposit. The stated deposit is 10 per cent, although frequently a lesser sum is accepted by the seller. The purpose of the deposit is a part payment of the purchase price. It is also a sign of commitment by the buyer, and it gives the seller some protection in the

event of the buyer not proceeding. As will be seen, one of the seller's remedies where there is a failure to complete by the buyer is to forfeit the deposit: SC 7.5.2.

It should be noted that if a deposit of less than 10 per cent is paid, or there is no deposit, then in the event of a completion notice (see Chapter 12, section 12.2) being served the full 10 per cent deposit becomes payable: SC 6.8.4.

Except on a sale by auction, the deposit is to paid by banker's draft or a solicitor's cheque: SC 2.2.1. If the cheque paid in respect of the deposit is dishonoured, the seller may treat the contract as discharged: SC 2.2.4.

The deposit is normally paid to the seller's solicitor. It is important to identify the capacity in which the deposit is paid. If it is paid to the seller's solicitor as 'agent for the seller', then the solicitor holds the deposit on behalf of the seller. The deposit may be used for the seller's benefit, eg as a deposit on another transaction, or to pay off a mortgage, and must be paid over to the seller if the seller requests. In the event of default by the seller, one of the buyer's remedies is return of the deposit which could be problematical if it has been handed to the solicitor as agent for the seller and he is no longer in possession of it. For this reason, the Standard Conditions state that the deposit is to be held by the seller's solicitor 'as stakeholder': SC 2.2.3. This means that the solicitor is the agent for both parties, holds the deposit in accordance with their joint instructions and can only deal with the deposit with the authority of both parties. It therefore affords a buyer much greater protection, but it means from the seller's point of view that he does not have access to the deposit for his own purposes. The solicitor/stakeholder is to hold the deposit for the purposes envisaged: in the event of completion, it forms part of the purchase price and can be paid to the seller; in the event of the buyer's default the seller receives the deposit; in the event of the seller's default the deposit is to be returned to the buyer. In many transactions, the seller will himself be buying a property and would wish to use the deposit he receives from his buyer in connection with his purchase. If the seller's solicitor receives the deposit as agent, this is possible. If however he receives it as stakeholder then this would not be possible as he is to hold the deposit on behalf of both parties. As this could cause inconvenience, the Standard Conditions permit a partial relaxation:

> 'SC 2.2.2 If before completion the seller agrees to buy another property in England and Wales for his residence, he may use all or any part of the deposit as a deposit in that transaction to be held on terms to the same effect as this condition and condition 2.2.3.
> 2.2.3 Any deposit or part of a deposit not being used in accordance with condition 2.2.2. is to be held by the seller's solicitor as stakeholder on terms that on completion it is paid to the seller with accrued interest.'

12. *Chattels.* If any sum is to be paid for chattels, then this is specified. It is not strictly necessary as contracts for the sale of chattels do not have to be in writing and they could be the subject of a separate transaction. For convenience however

those chattels being sold are identified. If the chattels are not dealt with it would seem that this does not mean that the contract would be void for failure to satisfy the terms of s2 Law of Property (Miscellaneous Provisions) Act 1989 and include all material terms, as the terms relating to chattels could be severed and would not affect the contract for the sale of land.

It must be emphasised that fixtures are not included. Unless the seller intends to sever a fixture, a fixture forms part of the land and passes automatically with the land and will be included in the description and price. What has to be specified here are those chattels which are not fixtures but which the buyer is acquiring, or those matters which are fixtures which the seller intends to sever prior to completion but is willing to sell. The issue of severance of fixtures needs to be addressed before contracts are exchanged, as the contractual description of the land will include any fixtures attached to it at the date of contract without specific reference. It is obviously desirable to clarify the issues of fixtures and fittings, what is included in the price, what is excluded, what the seller is keeping, etc. The Conveyancing Protocol documentation endeavours to achieve this. One of the documents is a fixtures and fittings form in which the seller specifies those items which he is taking, those included in the price and those available for purchase.

4.3 Special conditions

The above sets out the basic terms of the contract. Consideration then has to be given to the special conditions, ie those matters which relate to the particular transaction and for which specific provision needs to be made.

Some common special conditions are set out on the form in Appendix 2. They need not be used and may be deleted in any particular transaction.

1. This incorporates the Standard Conditions but makes plain that any express provision which is inconsistent with the Standard Conditions prevails.
2. This clause precludes any queries after exchange on the incumbrances which are specified in the contract. As the buyer has been given notice of the incumbrances, he should raise any queries at the pre-contract stage and only proceed to exchange once he is satisfied.
3. This confirms that the seller will transfer the property with the specified title guarantee.
4. This relates back to the price. In order to achieve certainty those chattels which are included in the sale – ie not the subject of a separate payment – are set out on an agreed list. The price for chattels on the front page is in relation to those which are not specifically included in the sale.
5. This needs to be completed in order to specify precisely what obligation the seller is undertaking. In the normal case, it is a contractual obligation that the

seller will deliver vacant possession of the property on the completion date. If he does not do so he is in breach. If the property is being sold subject to leases or tenancies, they must be specified and in due course notice will have to be served on the tenant to confirm the change of landlord.

There must then be included any provision relevant to the transaction. If for example in the conveyance new restrictive covenants are to be imposed, provision must be made for them here. If new easements are to be created, either in favour of the land sold or retained, again express provision should be included. Also, here is where clauses modifying or excluding the Standard Conditions would be included. If there are problems with the title, then a special condition should be included. For example, there may be a missing deed from the title deeds or for some reason a title less than 15 years is offered. The seller must deal with this by means of a condition and the buyer may require a defective title insurance policy to be provided, which again should be dealt with in a special condition. A buyer is entitled to copies of incumbrances such as restrictive covenants. If they were imposed a long time ago, it is quite possible that although they are known of a copy does not exist. Again, the property will be sold subject to them but the seller should insert a special condition stating that there are no details and no requisition or objection can be made for that lack. It is important that issues such as these are identified and dealt with in the contract as once the contract is made it is too late to do anything about them.

4.4 Void conditions

Although the general principle is freedom of contract there are exceptions in that by statute the following conditions if imposed are made void:

1. under s117 Stamp Act 1891, a condition preventing a buyer from objecting to an insufficiency of stamping on a document or requiring the buyer to pay for the stamping of such a document;
2. under s125 LPA, a condition preventing a buyer examining a power of attorney under which a document is executed;
3. under s48 LPA, any condition restricting the buyer in his choice of solicitor;
4. under s42 LPA, a condition that the purchaser must accept a title made with the concurrence of the owner of an equitable interest if that interest could be overreached, or a condition that the purchaser should pay towards the cost of appointing trustees.

5

Pre-contract Searches and Inquiries

5.1 Introduction

5.2 Searches

5.3 Inquiries and inspection

5.1 Introduction

Before contracts are concluded it is for the purchaser to satisfy himself as to the physical state and condition of the property and check that various legal matters are in order. These inquiries can broadly be divided into two categories:

1. Searches – investigations of public authorities.
2. Inquiries – other investigations carried out by the proposed purchaser.

The reason why these have to be done is that the basic principle of caveat emptor – let the buyer beware – applies.

Under an open contract the seller is under a very limited duty of disclosure. He is under a duty only to disclose latent defects in title, ie those defects in title which are not apparent on an inspection of the property such as some easements and restrictive covenants. His failure to disclose anything other than these to a purchaser will give the purchaser no recourse.

Under the Standard Conditions the position is different. Standard Condition 3 deals with matters affecting the property. (See Chapter 4, section 4.2 for a more detailed discussion of this.) Under SC 3.1.1 the seller agrees to sell the property free from incumbrances except those mentioned in Condition 3.1.2. The seller is therefore making it a term of the contract that the only incumbrances which will adversely affect the property are those specified in SC 3.1.2.

Standard Condition 3.1.2 states, inter alia, that the property is sold subject to entries made before the date of the contract in public registers, except those maintained by the Land Registry, the Land Charges Registry or Companies House. Searches therefore need to be carried out in various public registers as the buyer will be bound by them and will have no reason to complain of the seller as the contract specifically makes the sale subject to any matters registered.

5.2 Searches

Local search

Whether the land is registered or unregistered a purchaser must carry out a local search. This is effected by submitting the appropriate form to the relevant local authority for the area where the land is situated: the district council where there is a two-tier local authority, otherwise the unitary authority or borough council. The purpose of this search is to discover whether there are any entries affecting the property in the register of local land charges which these authorities have to keep under the Local Land Charges Act 1975. It should be noted that local land charges are registered against the land and not the estate owner as is the case with land charges under the LCA.

The local land charges register is divided into 12 parts and the following are the more common charges which may be registered:

Part 1 – General financial charges
Part 2 – Specific financial charges
Both of these enable a local authority which has expended money on various matters, such as street works, maintenance of sewers or drains, remedial works under planning or public health legislation, to register a charge against the property affected to secure the right of reimbursement.

Part 3 – Planning charges
In this part of the register appear entries relating to the planning history of the property – planning permissions, tree preservation orders, enforcement and stop notices.

Part 4 – Miscellaneous non-planning prohibitions and restrictions
Here will appear any other restrictions such as smoke control orders designating a smokeless zone and demolition orders.

Part 10 – Listed buildings
If the property is listed as a building of special architectural or historical interest it will be registered here

Part 11 – Light obstruction notices
These notional obstructions under the Rights of Light Act 1959 are registered here.

The result of the search takes the form of a certificate from the local authority with details of any matters registered. It should be noted that the certificate is only evidence of the state of the registers on the day it is given and unlike other searches confers no priority. However, as most local land charges relate to matters which do not come into existence rapidly this does not normally cause any problems. If a matter is to become a local land charge, then other investigations and inquiries will normally reveal that this is in progress.

Inquiries of local authorities

In addition to the matters referred to above, local authorities also possess information which is of interest to a prospective purchaser. Therefore, as well as the local search above, a purchaser will also make inquiries of the local authority. This is done by submitting a form containing standard inquiries, the form of which has been agreed between the Law Society and the local government organisations.

The form is divided into Parts 1 and 2. Part 1 contains the standard inquiries which are answered in all cases. They included matters such as:

1. drains and sewers (does the property drain to a public sewer and is any sewer maintainable at the public expense?);
2. roads (are the roads adjoining the property adopted and maintained at public expense?) and town and country planning issues (eg the status of development plans affecting the property);
3. smoke control area and compulsory purchase proposals.

These inquiries may reveal information about matters which are in the process of becoming registrable local land charges.

Part 2 inquires are those which have to be specifically asked to be answered. These include matters such as footpaths and pipelines affecting the property.

Index map search

If the land being sold has an unregistered title, an official search of the index map at the Land Registry should be carried out. This will reveal whether the title to the land is in fact registered and if it is it will give the title number. It will also reveal whether there is pending an application for first registration or whether a caution against first registration has been registered.

Commons registration search

Under the Commons Registration Act 1965 commons and town or village greens have to be registered. These are registered by the appropriate county council or London or borough council. Where appropriate a search should be made in these registers since if registered it is likely that there will be local public rights over the property.

Mining search

In areas affected by coal mining a mining search should be carried out at British

Coal. This will reveal the mining history and indicate whether the property could be affected by mining underneath it.

5.3 Inquiries and inspection

Introduction

As has been mentioned the open contract rule is caveat emptor, and under an open contract the seller gives no implied warranty as to the physical condition of the property or its suitability for any particular purpose. It is for the buyer to satisfy himself as to the physical state of the property, its suitability for his purpose and any other relevant matter.

Under the Standard Conditions, SC 3.2 is the main provision. Under SC 3.2.1 the buyer is to accept the property in the physical state it is in at the date of the contract unless the seller is building or converting it. This makes it plain that it is for the buyer to satisfy himself as to the physical state of the property at the date of the contract – whatever that may be – as that is the state in which he will have to accept it on completion. He cannot therefore complain about structural defects or problems which were present at the time the contract was concluded.

Inquiries of the seller

One source of information is the seller. As under an open contract the seller was under a very limited duty of disclosure the practice developed of the buyer asking the seller preliminary inquiries. Although it was not necessary to use them there were various printed forms containing standard inquiries. These asked the seller to give details of various factual issues – for example, confirmation of boundaries, who maintained fences, were mains services connected, were there any adverse rights affecting the property, who was in occupation, were there any disputes relating to the property, what was the planning history, were any fixtures and fitting included in the sale, etc. The practice developed of issuing increasing numbers of standard questions without specifically referring to the property. This was causing in many cases unreasonable and pointless work on the part of sellers to prepare replies. Accordingly under the Conveyancing Protocol the seller now prepares a property information form. As part of the pre-contract package the seller supplies standard information without being asked. This has removed the need for many preliminary inquiries, but it is always open to a purchaser to ask specific queries if he so wishes and of course if there is a particular matter on which information is needed specific inquiries must be made. Also, in cases where the Protocol is not being used, the old procedure can still be followed. The seller is under no obligation to answer any query put to him but obviously a refusal to answer a question would be, if nothing else, a matter of comment. Although a seller is under no duty to give information, if he does so he is under a duty to make sure that the information supplied is accurate. There is also a continuing duty imposed on the seller. If information true when given subsequently becomes incorrect, then that up-to-date information has to be passed on so that the purchaser is aware of the change. In *Corner* v *Mundy* [1987] CLY 479, for example, a seller stated in preliminary inquiries that the central heating was in good order, which it was. Before contracts were exchanged the water froze and caused damage This change was not told to the purchaser who was able to claim damages.

If a purchaser is unhappy with the information supplied, or finds that information given before exchange of contracts is incorrect, he can simply not proceed as at this stage in the transaction – he is not bound by any contract. If after exchange of contracts has taken place it is discovered that the pre-contract information supplied by the seller is incorrect then the purchaser may have remedies in misrepresentation: see Chapter 13.

Inspection

A physical inspection of the property should always be carried out. This may reveal matters not disclosed, such as discrepancies in boundaries or easements. It may also reveal whether there are persons in occupation other than the seller, and then the issue of what rights they may have in the property can be pursued. Under the rule in *Hunt* v *Luck* [1902] 1 Ch 428, a purchaser who does not carry out an inspection has constructive notice of the rights of a person in occupation which he would have discovered had he carried out an inspection.

The most important aspect of inspection however is for the buyer to satisfy himself as to the physical condition of the property because of SC 3.2.1 (above). In practice this means that the buyer should have a survey done.

If the purchaser is buying the property with mortgage finance then the lender will have a valuation done. This is a report by a valuer prepared for the lender and is designed to protect the lender's position as lender and to make sure that the property will be adequate security for the money which is to be lent. It is not designed to protect the purchaser's position as purchaser. It is now normal practice for the mortgage valuation to be disclosed to the purchaser, and in many cases this will be the only survey which is carried out. Although prepared for the lender it will in be relied on in many cases by the purchaser.

In *Yianni* v *Edwin Evans* [1982] QB 438 it was held that in these circumstances the building society valuer owed a duty of care to the borrower/purchaser and the borrower could rely on the report. It should however be noted that the duty owed depends on the nature of the survey. It is a valuation not a survey, and the inquiries which the valuer carries out are limited.

After *Yianni* v *Edward Evans* the practice developed of lenders including a disclaimer in valuations which were disclosed to the buyers stating that neither the lender nor the valuer accepted any liability towards the borrower/purchaser. The effectiveness of these disclaimers was considered by the House of Lords in *Smith* v *Eric S Bush; Harris* v *Wyre Forest District Council* [1989] 2 All ER 514. These cases involved properties at the lower end of the market. The mortgage valuations were disclosed to the purchasers and subsequently defects were found. In each case there was a disclaimer. The House of Lords held that the disclaimers could not be relied on as they failed the 'fair and reasonable' test under the Unfair Contract Terms Act 1977. It was known to all parties that the reports would be relied on and therefore the disclaimer did not prevail. There may however be cases where such a disclaimer could be upheld as being fair and reasonable – eg if the sum being lent was a small proportion of the purchase price, or if the purchaser was himself an expert (eg in *Stevenson* v *Nationwide Building Society* (1984) 272 EG 663 the purchaser was an estate agent who appreciated the nature of a valuation and what was being done; the disclaimer could be relied on by the lender).

The counsel of perfection in a conveyancing transaction will always be that a purchaser should commission his own independent survey. This will however put the purchaser to expense at a time when he is trying to keep expense to a minimum, hence the many cases where the lender's report is the only one prepared. An independent survey prepared for a buyer has several advantages over the lender's valuation. The surveyor will be acting for the purchaser and not the lender. The inspection will be more detailed, although precisely how detailed will depend on the actual nature of the survey requested. Also, there will be a contract between the purchaser and surveyor and any claim for a negligent survey will be in contract, whereas any claim against a lender's valuer is in the tort of negligence. It should be noted how damages are calculated for a defective survey. The measure of damages is the difference between the property as described in the report and the property as it actually is. The measure of damages is not the cost of the repairs: *Perry* v *Sidney Phillips & Son* [1982] 3 All ER 705. For example, in *Watts* v *Morrow* [1991] 4 All ER 937 following a survey the plaintiff bought a property for £177,500. Subsequently, defects were found and the cost of the repairs was nearly £34,000. The value of the property with the defects was £162,500. The trial judge awarded the cost of the repairs as damages. This was reversed by the Court of Appeal which stated that the damages were £15,000, ie the difference between the value of the property as described in the report   defect free, £177,500 – and the value of the property as it actually was – with the defects, £162,500. The logical conclusion of this approach is that if a purchaser buys a property after a survey which has been done negligently and does not reveal defects, but the property with the defects is actually worth the purchase price, then the purchaser has no claim against the surveyor (except for minor incidental expenses, of course).

Liability of a builder developer

It has already been mentioned that a developer owes a duty of care to prepare an accurate plan of property being sold. In addition, the caveat emptor rule has been modified somewhat in relation to builders/developers who build houses for sale. At common law, where a builder sold a house in the course of construction, there were implied terms that he would undertake the work in a good and workmanlike manner, would supply good and proper materials, and would ensure that the building would be reasonably fit for human occupation. Since 1974 builders of houses are subject to the Defective Premises Act 1972. This imposes on builders and other persons working in connection with the provision of a dwelling – including architects, subcontractors, surveyors and some suppliers of materials – a duty to ensure that the building work is done in a workmanlike manner, with proper materials so that the dwelling will be fit for habitation. This duty is owed to the original purchaser and any other person who acquires a legal or equitable interest in the property. A person who has no interest in the property cannot claim under the Act but must rely on any common law remedy

It should be noted that the Act does not apply to property which have the benefit of NHBC protection: see Chapter 11, section 11.5.

6

Exchange of Contracts

6.1 Introduction

6.2 Exchange by post

6.3 Exchange by telephone

6.1 Introduction

It is normal conveyancing practice for a contract to be prepared in duplicate. There is no requirement for this and it would be perfectly in order for there to be one contract signed by both parties but this is not usual.

A contract for the sale of land is normally concluded when contracts are exchanged. This involves a copy of the contract signed by the seller being received by the buyer and a copy signed by the buyer being received by the seller. The contract comes into existence when the contracts are exchanged and not until. In *Eccles* v *Bryant and Pollock* [1948] Ch 93, for example, the purchaser had sent his copy of the signed contract to the vendor's solicitor, who held the vendor's signed contract. The vendor changed his mind. The purchaser's action for specific performance failed as there had been no exchange.

It should be noted that a solicitor does not have implied authority to sign a contract on his client's behalf; if he is to sign a contract he must have express authority. Before exchange, both parts must be signed by the appropriate parties and it must be confirmed that both parts are identical. If they are not then no contract comes into existence. For example, in *Harrison* v *Battye* [1974] 3 All ER 830 one part of the contract had been amended to record a reduced deposit and the other copy had not. Exchange of the two copies in those circumstances would not bring a contract into existence. The parties' solicitors should also check that all pre-contract work has been done and there is nothing outstanding. Although solicitors do not have implied authority to sign contracts they do have implied authority to exchange contracts.

In *Commission for New Towns* v *Cooper* [1995] 2 All ER 929 the Court of Appeal confirmed that exchange of contracts was a procedure which was well known to conveyancers and which involved the exchange of identical copies of the same document. The Court was not prepared to find that an exchange of faxes confirming a previous agreement could amount to exchange of contracts for the purpose of s2 Law of Property (Miscellaneous Provisions) Act 1989 and that exchange of contracts should continue to be given the above meaning.

6.2 Exchange by post

The normal procedure is that the purchaser sends his part of the contract to the seller together with the deposit. On receipt of this the seller will post his part of the contract. When under an open contract a contract is concluded is open to some doubt – possibly when the second part of the contract is posted, or possibly when it is received. This doubt is resolved under the Standard Conditions and SC 2.1.1 states that if the contract is to be made by exchanging duplicate copies by post, the contract is made when the last copy is posted. In other words the postal rules relating to contract formation are applied.

6.3 Exchange by telephone

In *Domb* v *Isoz* [1980] Ch 548 the Court of Appeal confirmed that there could be an exchange of contracts without a physical exchange of documents. If each party's solicitor holds his own client's signed contract they can by telephone agree that contracts are exchanged and each will then hold his part of the contract on behalf of the other party. Standard Condition 2.1.2 confirms this, by stating that if the parties' solicitors agree to treat exchange as taking place before duplicate copies are actually exchanged, the contract will be made as agreed.

The Law Society has introduced three formulae to standardise procedures when there is a telephonic exchange.

Formula A

This is to be used where one party, normally the seller, holds both parts of the contract duly signed. Once a completion date is agreed, the solicitor holding both parts confirms that he holds his client's part and that both parts are identical. The solicitors agree that completion shall be treated as taking place. The solicitor then dates both parts and confirms that he holds his client's part of the contract to the other solicitor's order and undertakes to send his part of the contract forthwith.

Formula B

This is used when each solicitor holds his own client's part of the contract. Once a completion date is agreed each solicitor confirms that he holds his client's part of the contract, and they insert the completion date. Each undertakes to hold his signed part to the order of the other and contracts are exchanged at that moment. Each undertakes to deliver his part of the contract to the other party forthwith, and the purchaser's solicitor undertakes to send the deposit.

Formula C

This is used when there is a chain of linked transactions, each dependent on the other. It deals with the situation where person is buying a house and needs to sell his existing house in order to fund the purchase. In such a transaction, he wishes to avoid contracting to buy the new property when he has not contracted to sell, as he will in that situation be committed to two properties. Equally, he wishes to avoid contracting to sell his own house before contracting to buy, as he would in that situation have no house. He wishes to ensure that at any time he is committed to owning one property only. Formula C is designed to achieve that objective. Each buyer's solicitor gives an undertaking to his seller to exchange by a certain time if called upon to do so. These undertakings pass up the chain until there is an actual exchange, probably using formula A. Exchanges then follow. For example:

A is selling to B,
B is selling to C, and
C is selling to D.

D is the first time buyer who does not have a property to sell, and A is the end of the chain, selling but not buying. The chain begins by D's solicitor giving an undertaking to C's solicitor to exchange contracts if C's solicitor contacts him before 3.30 pm and calls upon him to do so. At this stage there is no exchange of contracts, but merely a commitment by D's solicitor to effect exchange if C's solicitor requires him to do so. If C does not contact him before 3.30 pm then there will be no exchange. C's solicitor then gives a similar undertaking to B's solicitor to exchange if called upon to do so by 3.00 pm. C's solicitor can give this undertaking because he holds D's solicitor's undertaking. Again, at this stage there is no contract between B and C. B's solicitor can now exchange with A in safety because he holds C's solicitor's undertaking to exchange. Having exchanged on the purchase, B's solicitor contacts C's solicitor and effects exchange in pursuance of the undertaking. C's solicitor then contacts D's solicitor and exchanges contracts on D's purchase.

This system is cumbersome and is not used a great deal in practice. It relies on solicitors giving undertakings which have to be honoured; if a solicitor's undertaking is not honoured that is professional misconduct which can result in a solicitor being struck off the Roll and ceasing to be able to practise.

7

The Position after Exchange

7.1 Introduction

7.2 Estate contract

7.3 Seller as trustee

7.4 Seller's position

7.5 Risk and insurance

7.6 Frustration

7.7 Possession by buyer pending completion

7.8 Death

7.9 Bankruptcy

7.1 Introduction

A contract for the sale of land is one of those contracts for which the remedy of specific performance may be available. This is an equitable remedy and as such is discretionary and will be granted on the basis of the applicable equitable principles. Because of the availability of specific performance and the maxim 'equity looks on that as done which ought to be done', once contracts are exchanged the status of the parties changes. In equity, provided that the contract is specifically enforceable, the purchaser is regarded as not merely having contractual rights but as having an equitable interest in the property.

7.2 Estate contract

In the case of unregistered land a contract for the purchase of land is an estate contract and is registrable as a Class C(iv) land charge under the Land Charges Act. If the land is registered then an estate contract is a minor interest which should be protected by registration of a notice or caution. However, in a routine transaction with a short time between exchange and completion a purchaser will not normally protect the contract by registration; in practice a contract will be so protected only if there is some specific reason for so doing, eg there is some fact which gives rise to suspicion or there is a long period between exchange and completion. In *Lake* v *Bayliss* [1974] 1 WLR 1073 it was held that if a seller contracts to sell to P1 and then actually conveys to P2, P2 takes free of P1's contract unless P1 has protected it by registration in the appropriate manner. In such a case, however, the seller would hold the proceeds of sale on trust for P1 who could trace into the proceeds of sale held by the seller.

7.3 Seller as trustee

If the contract is specifically enforceable then the seller becomes a sort of trustee for the purchaser who is in some sense a beneficiary. The seller cannot be regarded as a trustee in the normal sense of the word because, for example, he is entitled to occupy the property for his own purposes until completion; if the property is let the seller will be able to retain rent until completion. A normal trustee is not entitled to use trust property for his own purpose but has to use it for the benefit of the beneficiary.

7.4 Seller's position

The seller is entitled to retain possession until completion or retain the rent if the property is let. The seller has a duty of care towards the property and must manage it with the same degree of care as a trustee owes to his beneficiaries. He must protect it physically. He must maintain it in a reasonable state of preservation and insofar as possible in the state it was at the date of the contract. The seller must bear the cost of maintenance and is not entitled to recover the cost from the purchaser.

 The seller must also take care in the management of the property so as to have regard to the purchaser's interests. For example, a seller should not determine a tenancy without the purchaser's agreement nor should he create new tenancies after exchange without the purchaser's agreement: *Abdulla* v *Shah* [1959] AC 124.

 Where property is sold subject to a lease, the position is regulated by SC 3.3.2:

'a) ...
b) The seller is to inform the buyer without delay if the lease ends or if the seller learns of any application by the tenant in connection with the lease; the seller is then to act as the buyer reasonably directs, and the buyer is to indemnify the seller against all consequent loss and expense
c) The seller is not to agree to any proposal to change the lease terms without the consent of the buyer and is to inform the buyer without delay of any change which may be proposed or agreed'.

The seller's duty of care continues after contractual completion date if completion is delayed for some reason, so long as the seller remains in possession.

The seller has a lien on the property as security for the purchase price or any outstanding balance. This lien remains enforceable while there is money outstanding even if the sale has been completed and the purchaser is in occupation. Such a lien should be protected by registration as a Class C(iii) land charge or by notice or caution if it is to be enforceable against third parties.

7.5 Risk and insurance

The open contract position

Under an open contract the risk passes to the purchaser on exchange and he then has the obligation to insure. Even if buildings are destroyed the seller can still convey the legal estate in the land and the purchaser will remain liable for the full purchase price. The seller is under no obligation to insure but if he does so the purchaser may have a claim on the insurance money. There are statutory provisions which deal with this issue, but reliance on them is not regarded as satisfactory.

Under s47 LPA, if the seller has maintained his insurance, and after exchange money becomes payable under the policy in respect of damage or destruction to the property, the money shall on completion be held by the seller on trust for the purchaser. This section can be excluded by the contract (SC 5.1.4 does so, see below), is subject to the purchaser paying a proportionate part of the premium and requires the insurance company to consent – most insurance companies will recognise the interest of a purchaser.

Under s83 Fires Prevention Metropolis Act 1774 if property is damaged by fire the insurance company is required to reinstate the property if requested to do so by a person with an interest in the property.

Under the Standard Conditions

The position under the Standard Conditions is different and risk and insurance are dealt with in SC 5.1.

> 'SC 5.1.1 The seller will transfer the property in the same physical state as it was at the date of the contract (except for fair wear and tear), which means that the seller retains the risk until completion.
> 5.1.2. If at any time before completion the physical state of the property makes it unusable for its purpose at the date of the contract
> a) the buyer may rescind the contract
> b) the seller may rescind the contract where the property has become unusable for that purpose as a result of damage against which the seller could not reasonably have insured or which it is not legally possible for the seller to make good.

5.1.3. The seller is under no obligation to the buyer to insure the property.

5.1.4. Section 47 of the Law of Property Act 1925 does not apply.'

The effect of these provisions is that the property is not at the buyer's risk after exchange of contracts and the buyer does not have to insure. Equally, the seller does not have to insure but the property remains at his risk and he has a contractual obligation to transfer the property in the same condition it was at the date of the contract. If the property is damaged after exchange the buyer can claim damages from the seller; if the property is destroyed the purchaser can rescind and claim damages from the seller.

7.6 Frustration

After a long period of doubt is has been held that the doctrine of frustration can apply to leases, although it will be extremely rare that it will do so: *National Carriers Ltd* v *Panalpina (Northern) Ltd* [1981] AC 675. Where a contract for the sale of land has been completed and the legal estate has passed to the purchaser obviously frustration cannot apply. In relation to an uncompleted contract, it has been assumed that frustration could apply to a contract for the sale of land – *Amalgamated Investment and Property Co Ltd* v *John Walker and Sons Ltd* [1976] 3 All ER 509 – although on the facts there was no frustration. In that case after exchange of contracts the property was listed as a building of exceptional historic or architectural importance which had the effect of preventing the development which the purchaser intended to carry out. The Court of Appeal indicated that frustration could apply but on the facts did not. In practice it will be extremely rare for frustration to apply to a contract for the sale of land. Where the Standard Conditions apply, SC 5.1 deals with the issue of damage, and it should also be noted that under SC 3.1.2(e) the property is sold subject to public requirements, defined in SC 1.1.1(j) as 'any notice, order or proposal given or made (whether before or after the date of the contract) by a body acting on statutory authority.' Thus, the listing above would not give the buyer any remedy, nor for example would a compulsory purchase order.

7.7 Possession by buyer pending completion

The seller is entitled to retain possession until completion. Therefore, if the buyer is to take possession before completion it can only be with the agreement of the seller, either under the contract or otherwise. From the seller's point of view it is something which always has to be carefully considered since if the buyer is in occupation and does not complete then the seller has to take steps to remove him.

Under an open contract the buyer going into possession before completion was hazardous for both parties. The purchaser became a tenant at will, agreed to pay interest and became responsible for repairs. He also, by taking possession, waived his right to object to defects in title. As the purchaser became a tenant at will, then he could in some circumstances have obtained security of tenure under the Rent Acts or Housing Acts.

Standard Condition 5.2 deals with this in contracts to which the Standard Conditions apply. Under SC 5.2.1 if the buyer is let into occupation the buyer is a licensee not a tenant. The terms of the licence under SC 5.2.2 are:

1. it is not transferable;
2. members of the buyer's household may occupy the property;
3. the buyer takes responsibility for all outgoings and expenses and is to indemnify the seller;
4. the buyer will pay a fee calculated at the contract rate on the balance of purchase price outstanding;
5. the buyer can keep any rents or profits;
6. the buyer is to keep the property is as good a state of repair as it was when he went into occupation (fair wear and tear excepted);
7. the buyer is to insure the property for not less than the purchase price;
8. the buyer will vacate when the licence terminates.

On the creation of the buyer's licence SC 5.1 ceases to apply and the buyer assumes the risk until completion: SC 5.2.3.

The buyer's licence comes to an end on the earliest of completion date, rescission of the contract or the expiry of five day's notice given by either party. It is made quite clear in SC 5.2.4 that the buyer is not in occupation if he merely exercises rights of access to carry out work agreed by the seller.

Finally, under SC 5.2.7, a buyer by taking up occupation does not waive his right to object to defects in title and raise requisitions – a reversal of the open contract situation.

7.8 Death

The death of neither the seller nor the buyer discharges the contract, which has to be completed although the relevant legal formalities consequent on the death will cause delay and may mean that the contractual completion date will not be met.

If a sole seller dies, then his personal representatives have to obtain the appropriate grant of representation and then complete. If a trustee or co-owner who is selling dies, then the transaction can continue, subject to there being two trustees to give a receipt. If there is only one trustee remaining (unless a trust corporation) it will be necessary to appoint a new trustee in order for the conveyance to overreach any equitable interests.

If a purchaser dies then his personal representatives have to complete.

7.9 Bankruptcy

Introduction

Bankruptcy is now governed by the Insolvency Act 1986. Bankruptcy proceedings are commenced by a petition and an order is then made. A person becomes bankrupt on the day the order is made, and in due course a trustee in bankruptcy will be appointed. On appointment all the bankrupt's assets vest automatically in the trustee.

If the seller becomes bankrupt his assets vest in the trustee who will be bound to complete the sale, subject to his power to disclaim onerous property: s315 Insolvency Act 1986. This power enables a trustee to disclaim property which is unprofitable or unsaleable, and it includes contracts. For the power to be exercisable, the contract must be unprofitable or onerous; a trustee cannot disclaim merely because he does not wish to proceed with the contract and wishes to sell elsewhere. A purchaser from a trustee should check the bankruptcy order and the trustee's appointment. Where there is a sale following a bankruptcy the purchase money must be paid to the trustee and not the bankrupt.

If the purchaser goes bankrupt, the trustee can either complete the contract or he can disclaim it under the power referred to above.

Registration

The bankruptcy petition and the bankruptcy order will be registered against the bankrupt under the LCA, with the usual consequence that registration is notice and a purchaser in good faith is not bound by these matters if they are not registered. These registrations are effected whether or not the bankrupt owns land, and if he does whether or not the land is registered. If the bankrupt owns registered land then a notice will be registered on presentation of the petition, and on the making of the bankruptcy order a bankruptcy inhibition will be registered preventing all dealings with the land. Under the Insolvency Act 1986 title to the land vests in the trustee automatically without any entry being made in the register.

8

Deduction and Investigation of Title

8.1 Introduction

8.2 Registered land

8.3 Unregistered title

8.1 Introduction

The deduction and investigation of title are similar concepts and are sides of the same coin.

Deduction of title is the process whereby the seller proves to the purchaser that he has a good title and that he can transfer the property in accordance with the contract. In order to do this the seller will have to check the title deeds and documentation and prepare evidence to be supplied to the buyer. The process of investigating title is the process where the buyer checks the evidence supplied by the seller to make sure that it does indeed accord with the contract and raises queries by means of requisitions on title if there are matters with which he is not happy. Traditionally, these two activities took place after exchange of contracts. More recently, and particularly in the light of the Protocol, these matters are dealt with as part of the pre-contract stage, so that contracts now will not be exchanged unless and until the purchaser is satisfied with the title.

8.2 Registered land

The position concerning registered land is relatively simple. Under SC 4.2 the evidence of title which has to be produced by the seller is office copies of the entries on the register.

Investigation of title is much simpler in that it involves checking the office copies to make sure that they are satisfactory and, in due course, transferring the property by reference to the entries on the register.

It should be noted however that the register is not exhaustive; in particular the land is subject to overriding interests, which do not appear on the register, so evidence of overriding interests needs to be checked, eg the interest of an occupier under s70(1)(g) LRA.

If there is a restriction in the proprietorship register, eg if the land is vested in trustees, then the procedure there defined must be followed.

8.3 Unregistered title

Introduction

The seller deduces title in unregistered land by delivering evidence of his title to the purchaser. This will either be an abstract, the traditional form, which is a written summary of the deeds, documents and events affecting the land, or an epitome which consists of photocopy deeds and documents accompanied by an index setting out in brief form the history of the land: see the example in Appendix 3. (Henceforth in this chapter both of these will be referred to as an abstract.) The purchaser then investigates the title by checking the evidence supplied and ensuring that it is satisfactory and in accordance with the contract. If the buyer is not satisfied then he raises inquiries with the seller by means of requisitions on title. These are formal requests by the buyer to the seller for information or for problems with the title to be resolved.

The open contract rule is contained in s44(1) LPA as amended by s23 LPA 1969. Between 1925 and 1969, a seller had to produce evidence of title going back at least 30 years; in 1969 this period was reduced to a minimum of 15 years.

As part of the process of investigating title, a purchaser should ensure that all documents have been stamped for stamp duty purpose.

Root of title

The title has to be traced from a good root of title. This is a document which is at least 15 years old, and the devolution of the property then has to be traced from the root, showing all events and changes of ownership down to the seller. A good root of title is not defined by statute, nor is there any case defining it. The Law Commission accepted the definition in *Williams on Vendor and Purchaser* (4th edn, 1936), that a good root of title is:

> '... an instrument of disposition dealing with or proving on the face of it, without the aid of extrinsic evidence, the ownership of the whole legal and equitable estate in the property sold, containing a description by which the property can be identified and showing nothing to cast any doubt on the title of the disposing person.'

It is normal for the root of title to be a conveyance on sale since if there was a sale it is presumed that on that occasion the purchaser investigated the title properly, so that the title period then investigated can in effect be added on to the period supplied by the vendor. Other documents such as assents, deeds of gift and mortgages can be a good root but in practice a conveyance on sale will be the norm.

The contract specifies the root of title. The open contract rule now contained in s44(1) LPA specifies a minimum period of 15 years, and this will be the period which will apply unless the contract itself specifies some other period. A purchaser may accept a root of title less than 15 years old by virtue of a special condition in the contract, but if he does so he is at risk for the following reasons:

1. he will have constructive notice of any equitable interest he would have discovered had he investigated the title for the full period;
2. a land charge may have been registered against the name of an estate owner which the short title does not reveal but which an investigation of the full title would have revealed. The purchaser will take subject to this land charge but will not be able to claim compensation under the LPA 1969.

Deduction of title

Once the root of title has been fixed, the seller has to trace the devolution of the property to himself with no gaps or defects. The documents which should be abstracted, ie evidence of which should be produced to the buyer, include conveyances, deeds of gift, mortgages both subsisting and discharged, evidence of discharge of mortgages, subsisting leases, leases which have come to an end otherwise than by effluxion of time, assents, grants of probate and letters of administration, deeds of retirement and appointment of trustees, powers of attorney and memoranda endorsed on any deed or document. Events which should be abstracted and of which appropriate evidence should be supplied include marriages (if change of name), changes of name and deaths. There is no requirement that Land Charge Registry certificates be abstracted but in practice they usually will be. There is no requirement to abstract wills if the deceased died after 1925. In such a case the legal title passes from the deceased to the personal representatives whose title derives from the grant of probate or letters of administration. Nor should any equitable interest which will be overreached on the sale be abstracted: s10 LPA. On a sale by a mortgagee, evidence that the power of sale is exercisable does not have to be abstracted, merely evidence that the power of sale has arisen: see Chapter 9, section 9.3. Although one of the main objectives of the 1925 legislation was to make the legal estate the basis of conveyancing and prevent the need to investigate equitable interests, there may be occasions when equitable interests have to be brought onto the title. For example, if A and B own property as equitable tenants in common and B dies leaving his half share to A in his will, A becomes the sole owner and is able to sell. To prove that however the will and the devolution of the equitable interests would have to be abstracted.

Pre-root documents

Under s45(1) LPA the general rule is that the seller does not have to abstract nor is the purchaser entitled to ask for or raise requisitions on documents prior to the root of title.

There are exceptions to this general principle, however. The seller does have to abstract the following pre-root documents and the buyer is entitled to ask for them:

1. Any power of attorney granted before the root of title under which any abstracted document is executed.
2. Any document creating an interest which has not expired and subject to which any part of the property is disposed of by an abstracted instrument. Thus, if the root of title is a conveyance dated 1950, but the sale to the purchaser will take effect subject to restrictive covenants contained in a 1930 conveyance, the 1930 conveyance has to be abstracted so that the purchaser can verify the terms of the covenants. Under this provision also it is considered that if the property is defined by reference to a plan on a pre-root document that pre-root plan has to be abstracted.
3. Any document creating a limitation or trust by reference to which any part of the property is disposed of by an abstracted document.

9

Investigating and Deducing Title – Particular Problems

9.1 Trustees

9.2 Co-owners

9.3 Mortgages

9.4 Personal representatives

9.5 Charities

9.6 Persons under a disability

9.7 Attorneys

9.8 Voluntary dispositions

9.1 Trustees

Introduction

Prior to 1997, land held in trust could be held either under a strict settlement under the Settled Land Act 1925, or upon trust for sale. The Trusts of Land and Appointment of Trustees Act (TOLATA) 1996 has altered the law. By s2, no new strict settlements can be created, although existing settlements continue. Section 1 introduces the new concept of the trust of land which is defined as any trust in relation to which the trust property is or includes land. As the definition applies to trusts in existence on 1 January 1997, existing trusts for sale now come under the new regime of trusts of land. There can be no more than four trustees of land, and they hold the legal estate as joint tenants upon trust for the beneficiaries. A purchaser is not concerned with the equitable interests. A purchaser from trustees needs to ensure that there are at least two trustees or that a sole trustee is a trust corporation in order to ensure that the equitable interests under the trust are overreached. When a purchaser is buying trust property he is concerned to trace the devolution of the legal estate. This means that he has to check deeds of appointment and retirement and deaths of trustees. As the legal estate is held by the trustees as joint tenants, the right of survivorship applies, and if a trustee has died all that needs to be produced is evidence of the death – usually a death certificate. As a general rule, the power of appointing new trustees is vested in the continuing trustees: s36 Trustee Act 1925 (unless the trust instrument confers this power on someone else). It should be noted that when the last surviving trustee dies, his personal representatives do not become the trustees but have the statutory power of appointment, so they have to appoint new trustees to enable the land to be dealt with. On a sale, provided that the purchase money is paid to two trustees or a single trust corporation, the equitable interests under the trust will be overreached and the purchaser takes free of them whether or not he has notice.

Consents

It was always possible where there was a trust for sale under the LPA to make any sale subject to the consent of a specified person or persons. This provision is repeated in s10 TOLATA. If trustees can only exercise their power of sale with the consent of specified persons, they will be in breach of trust if they do not comply precisely with the terms as to consent and obtain all consents. Since such a provision could in effect prevent a sale the TOLATA repeats the provision in the LPA, that in favour of a purchaser the consent of any two specified persons is sufficient. Thus a purchaser only needs to ensure that two consents to a sale have been given, even if the trust documentation specifies more. (If any such person is a minor, then his consent is not required but the consent of a person with parental responsibility suffices.)

Protection of purchasers

TOLATA imposes certain duties on trustees of land when they are exercising their functions – to consider the position of beneficiaries (s6(5)), before partitioning trust property to obtain beneficiaries' consents (s7(3)), and to consult with beneficiaries: s11(1). A purchaser from trustees is not concerned to see that those requirements have been carried out and need not therefore investigate these issues: s16(1). If any transaction by trustees of land contravenes any court order or rule of law or equity then that does not invalidate the transaction unless the purchaser has actual notice of the contravention: s16(2). Subject to any contrary intention expressed in the trust instrument, under s6 TOLATA trustees of land have in relation to the land all the powers of an absolute owner, and under s7 they have a power to partition land between beneficiaries. Under s16(3), where trustees powers are limited by the trust documentation they are under a duty to take all reasonable steps to bring the limitation to the notice of a purchaser from them, but the limitation does not invalidate any conveyance to a purchaser unless he has actual notice of the limitation (although vis-à-vis the beneficiaries, again the trustees would be in breach of trust).

Delegation by trustees

The basic rule of equity has been that a trustee has to act in person and cannot delegate his functions. This rule is subject to exceptions and particular care needs to be taken when dealing with conveyances of trust property if these provisions are used. The trust instrument itself may authorise delegation and if all the beneficiaries are sui juris they may authorise the delegation. These are self explanatory. Delegation is also possible under s9 TOLATA, the Trustee Delegation Act 1999 and s25 Trustee Act 1925.

Section 9 TOLATA

Under s29 LPA, trustees for sale could delegate their powers of management to a beneficiary but not other powers. Section 9 TOLATA replaces s29. By using the powers in s9 it may be possible in many respects in a trust of land to recreate the position which obtained under a Settled Land Act settlement with a tenant for life, although unlike a strict settlement the legal estate under a trust of land will always remain vested in the trustees. Under s9(1) trustees of land may, by power of attorney, delegate to a beneficiary of full age and beneficially entitled to an interest in possession any of their trustee functions relating to the land, including the power of sale. All trustees must concur and the power must be given jointly, and it may be revoked by any one trustee. Any such delegation is automatically revoked if a new trustee is appointed, but not if a trustee dies or ceases to be a trustee since in these situations the principle of unanimity is not breached as all continuing trustees continue to authorise the delegation. The delegation may be for a specific period, or for an indefinite period, in which case it will last until revoked or a new trustee is appointed. If a beneficiary ceases to have an interest in possession, the power will be revoked automatically.

There are two particularly significant aspects of this provision for conveyancing. Delegation by power of attorney of trustees' powers is authorised in favour of a beneficiary with an interest in possession in the trust property. In order to check that the delegation is valid a person dealing with a beneficiary would have to check that the beneficiary had an interest in possession under the trust which would involve investigating the equitable interests, something which is to be avoided. In order to resolve this in favour of a person dealing with such a beneficiary, it will be presumed that he is a beneficiary with an interest in possession and that the delegation is valid unless the person dealing with the beneficiary had actual knowledge that the delegation was not authorised. This maintains the basic conveyancing principle that a purchaser should not normally have to be concerned with equitable interests. In favour of a purchaser whose title depends on the validity of the transaction between the beneficiary and the other person, it will be conclusively presumed that that other person acted in good faith and without notice that the delegation was not authorised if he makes a statutory declaration to that effect either before or within three months of the purchase. Under s9(7) it is made quite clear that the delegation effected under the above cannot extend to the receipt of capital money. Thus, if trustees delegate all their powers under s9(1) to a beneficiary on a sale by him, for the overreaching machinery to take effect the purchase money must still be paid to the trustees – being at least two or a trust corporation – and not to the beneficiary/delegate.

Trustee Delegation Act 1999

Under s25 Trustee Act 1925 a trustee could delegate his powers or functions by power of attorney for a period not exceeding 12 months. Such delegation had to be by a trust power of attorney and not by an ordinary power of attorney under the Powers of Attorney Act 1971. This power has been replaced by much wider powers under the Trustee Delegation Act 1999, where a trustee has a beneficial interest in the trust. Under s1 of the 1999 Act a trustee who has a beneficial interest in a trust of land can by power of attorney delegate all his trustee functions. In such a case, a general power of attorney under s10 Powers of Attorney Act 1971 will, unless the power itself or the trust documentation contain provisions to the contrary, operate to confer on the attorney all the donor's powers and functions as trustee. For such a delegation to be valid under this provision, the donor of the power must be a trustee with a beneficial interest under the trust. Under s2 of the 1999 Act, in favour of a purchaser an 'appropriate statement' is conclusive evidence that the donor of the power had such an interest. An appropriate statement is a statement signed by the donee of the power, either when doing an act or within three months of the act that at the time the act was done the donor had a beneficial interest. This provision maintains the basic conveyancing principle that a purchaser should not normally be concerned to investigate equitable interests.

Section 25 Trustee Act 1925

Section 5 of the Trustee Delegation Act 1999 inserts a redrafted s25 into the Trustee Act 1925. Under this any trustee may, by power of attorney, delegate the exercise of his powers and discretions for a maximum period of 12 months and the Act sets out a new statutory form of a Trustee Power of Attorney. Provided that the power is in that form or similar, and is expressed to be made under s25(2) of the Trustee Act 1925, it will delegate to the named person the donor's specified trustee functions. Any power must be given by a single donor to a single donee and relate to a single trust. In order to ensure that there will always be at least two trustees to receive capital money and ensure overreaching, s7 of the 1999 Act states that where a trustee has delegated his powers by a power of attorney under s25, one person cannot act as trustee and attorney, or as attorney for two or more trustees, unless there is another person acting with him.

9.2 Co-owners

Under the LPA co-ownership had to exist under a trust for sale. Whether land was held by joint tenants or tenants in common, if the conveyancing documents did not establish it the LPA imposed a trust for sale. Under TOLATA, where there is co-ownership, the land will be held under a trust of land, again either express or implied. Where there is co-ownership, as the legal estate will held by the trustees upon trust for the beneficiaries the general issues relating to trustees outlined above will apply. There are, however, further issues which need to be addressed in relation to co-owners.

Where there are two trustees, then a purchaser need not be concerned with equitable interests as they will be overreached. If the land is registered, then following *City of London Building Society* v *Flegg* [1986] Ch 605 the principle of overreaching prevails over that of overriding interests. In many cases, however, where there is co-ownership it may be the case that the legal estate is vested in one person, as trustee for himself and a third party. In such a case a sale by the sole trustee will not overreach equitable interests; in unregistered land the purchaser will take the land subject to equitable interests of which he has notice (*Kingsnorth Finance* v *Tizard* [1986] 2 All ER 54) and if the land is registered then there may be an overriding interest: eg *Williams and Glyn's Bank Ltd* v *Boland* [1981] AC 487. In order to avoid this situation a purchaser should at the pre-contract stage investigate to see whether there are any occupiers not on the deeds and if there are then steps could be taken to avoid problems, eg by ensuring that a non-owning occupier joins in the contract.

A particular problem is a sale by a surviving co-owner. The legal estate will always be vested in the trustees as joint tenants. If they are also beneficial joint tenants the right of survivorship applies to the equitable interest as well.

For example, A, B and C are trustees upon trust for themselves as beneficial joint tenants. C dies. The right of survivorship applies and A and B hold the legal estate upon trust for themselves as beneficial joint tenants. If B dies, the right of survivorship again applies and A becomes the sole legal and beneficial owner and the trust has come to an end. Death certificates will be produced to prove the deaths of B and C: see s36(2) LPA, added by the Law of Property (Amendment) Act 1926.

If, however, there is an equitable tenancy in common then there is no right of survivorship and the situation is different. For example, A, B and C are trustees upon trust for themselves as equitable tenants in common. C dies. The right of survivorship applies to the legal estate, and A and B will be the trustees holding upon trust for themselves and C's estate. As there are two trustees, A and B could still sell and overreach the equitable interests. If B dies, the legal estate will now be held by A alone, upon trust for himself, B's estate and C's estate. As A is a sole trustee a sale by him will not overreach the equitable interests From the point of view of a purchaser from A, if the title documents disclose the above then a purchaser can take appropriate steps. For example, if the conveyance to A, B and C stated that they held the property as beneficial joint tenants, then a purchaser would know that he faced the first situation above. If the conveyance stated that they held as beneficial tenants in common, a purchaser from A would know that he faced the situation outlined in the second case and could insist on the appointment of a second trustee. A problem was identified, however. If the conveyancing documentation stated that there was a joint tenancy, but there had in fact been a severance, the survivor would not be solely and beneficially entitled. For example, A and B bought property as beneficial joint tenants. B then severed the joint tenancy in equity by serving a notice on A. B then died. A would then hold the property on trust for himself and B's estate, but a purchaser would not discover this. Accordingly, in 1964, the Law of Property (Joint Tenants) Act remedied this. In favour of a purchaser the survivor of two or more joint tenants is deemed to be solely and beneficially entitled if he conveys as beneficial owner or the conveyance contains a statement that he is so entitled. The Act does not apply however if a notice of severance is indorsed on or annexed to the conveyance to the joint tenants. In such a case the purchaser will have notice of the position and will able to request that a second trustee be appointed.

Bankruptcy severs a joint tenancy by operation of law: see, eg, *Re Dennis (A Bankrupt)* [1995] 3 WLR 367. If a bankruptcy order has been registered against any of the joint tenants under the LCA a purchaser will have notice of that fact and can act appropriately. If not registered, then a purchaser does not have notice and need not concern himself further.

The 1964 Act does not apply to registered land. If the title to land is registered a purchaser will purchase by reference to the register. If there has been a severance then a restriction or caution could be registered. In the absence of such then a purchaser simply relies in the register (subject of course to there being an overriding interest). Thus, if A and B are registered as joint proprietors and B dies, then a purchaser can assume that A is able to sell unless there is a restriction or caution and subject to there being no overriding interest.

9.3 Mortgages

A mortgage charges the legal estate of the mortgagor. It is therefore necessary for a purchaser to check that any mortgages have been paid off because if they have not been they will continue to bind the land after the purchaser has acquired it. In unregistered land a purchaser needs to ensure that any mortgage in the title has been redeemed. If the seller owns the property subject to a mortgage then the purchaser needs to ensure that satisfactory arrangements are in place for the mortgage to be redeemed on completion. (This will normally be done by the seller's solicitor giving an undertaking to discharge the mortgage.) In unregistered land a vacating receipt is normally indorsed on the mortgage deed. In registered land Form DS1 is used, which is a form signed by the mortgagee confirming to the Land

Registry that the charge has been redeemed and any entry on the register can be cancelled. If there are puisne mortgages registered as Class C(i) land charges or equitable mortgages registered as Class C(iii) land charges, then when they are redeemed any entry at the Land Charges Registry also needs to be cancelled. In any mortgage made by deed there will be implied a power of sale in favour of the mortgagee: s101 LPA. After 1925, where there is a mortgage of freehold land the fee simple remains vested in the mortgagor, and the mortgagee either has a long lease or now, more usually, a legal charge. The power of sale enables a mortgagee to sell the legal estate which he does not in fact own.

The power of sale arises when the mortgage money is due, ie when the legal date for redemption has passed. It is exercisable in the circumstances set out in s103 LPA, if:

1. notice requiring repayment of the mortgage money has been served and default has been made for at least three months;
2. interest is at least two months in arrear;
3. there has been a breach of some other provision in the mortgage.

A purchaser from a mortgagee only has to check that the power of sale has arisen – ie that the legal date for redemption has passed. He is not concerned to see that the power of sale is exercisable. Whether the power of sale is exercisable is a matter to be resolved between the mortgagor and mortgagee and does not concern a purchaser. The effect of a sale by a mortgagee is to transfer the mortgaged estate free from the mortgage and all matters to which the mortgage has priority but subject to matters which have priority to the mortgage. As the mortgage has to be subsisting for the power of sale to be exercised, where there is a sale by a mortgagee there will not be a vacating receipt or, in registered land, a Form DS1.

For example, A mortgages land to M1, M2 and M3. He defaults. If M1 sells, he will sell the land free from M2's and M3's mortgages, although he has to hand any surplus on to M2. If M2 sells, the land will be transferred free of M3's mortgage but subject to M1's mortgage. In effect this means that M2 can only sell if he first repays M1 before taking any money from the sale in reduction of his own liabilities. M3 can only sell subject to the two earlier mortgages.

9.4 Personal representatives

Introduction

When a person dies leaving a will which appoints executors, the executors will apply for a grant of probate. This is official confirmation that the will is valid and that the executors are appointed. If a person dies without leaving a will, or if there is a will but no executor, then certain persons may apply for a grant of letters of administration. An executor's title derives from the will and the property vests in him on death, although he cannot deal with it until the grant is made. The title of an administrator derives from the grant. In relation to deaths after 1 July 1995, when a person dies intestate, until a grant is made, his property vests in the Public Trustee; prior to that the property vested in the President of the Family Division.

Executors and administrators together are called personal representatives. They generally have all the powers of trustees, and provisions of, for example, the Trustee Act 1925 and TOLATA apply to personal representatives, although they are not trustees stricto sensu. Unlike trustees however, there is no need for there to be two personal representatives. A single personal representative can sell property and give a good receipt, but if there are two or more personal representatives appointed, then they must all sign any contract for the sale of land and all must join in a conveyance.

Assents

When a person dies, his property devolves on his personal representatives, whose title is completed by the grant of probate or administration. (There are some exceptions to this – for example, jointly owned property passes by survivorship and does not devolve on the personal representatives.) A beneficiary under a will obtains no title to any asset through the will. Personal representatives are given wide powers to deal with the deceased's assets, eg a power to sell. Their functions are essentially threefold: to bring the deceased's assets under their control; to pay debts and liabilities; and, only when those are discharged, to distribute to the persons entitled. It may be that discharging liabilities exhausts the estate and in that case the beneficiaries will receive nothing.

Under s36(1) Administration of Estates Act (AEA) 1925 a personal representative may assent to the vesting in any beneficiary of any estate or interest in real estate (defined to include equitable interests, mortgages and leases (s3 AEA 1925)) to which the deceased was entitled before his death and which devolves on the personal representative. This means property which the deceased owned at the date of his death and does not include property which comes into the estate after death, eg if the deceased had contracted to buy land before his death and his personal representatives completed the purchase after his death, such land should be transferred to a beneficiary by means of a conveyance not an assent: *Re Stirrup's Contract* [1961] 1 All ER 805.

Section 36 refers to an assent to any person entitled by 'devise, bequest, devolution, appropriation or otherwise.' It is generally taken to mean that the words 'or otherwise' are to be interpreted eiusdem generis and apply to dealings in the course of administration. If the personal representatives sell, then an assent is not made to the purchaser but a conveyance or transfer is used.

The assent operates to vest the estate or interest in the person to whom it is made: s36(2).

An assent relating to a legal estate must be in writing, signed by the personal representatives and must name the person in whose favour it is made and it vests the legal estate in the named person. It should be noted that an assent relating to a legal estate does not have to be in a deed.

Insofar as property is an equitable interest an assent can still be informal and need not be in writing. For example, in *Re Edwards Will Trusts* [1982] Ch 30 the wife owned a house. She died intestate and her husband became entitled to it under the intestacy rules. He obtained a grant of letters of administration but did not assent to himself. He lived in the house for several years until his death. It was held that there was an implied assent in his own favour, inferred from conduct, of the equitable interest so that on his death he owned the beneficial interest which passed to his personal representatives.

Re King's Will Trusts *[1964] Ch 542*

If a will establishes a trust, and the executors are to be the trustees, this decision makes it plain that the personal representatives have to assent to themselves in order to change the capacity in which they hold the land. Without an assent they continue to hold as personal representatives and not as trustees. In *Re King's Will Trusts* A and B were appointed executors and trustees under the will of the deceased. B died and A purported to appoint C as a new trustee. It was held that the appointment was ineffective and did not vest any legal estate in C. B was a personal representative and not a trustee and therefore he did not have the statutory power of appointing new trustees. A should first have assented himself in order to change his capacity from that of personal representative to trustee and he could then have exercised the power.

Similarly, if a personal representative is a beneficiary, he needs to assent to himself in order to complete the title.

It must however be emphasised that if personal representatives in the course of administration wish to sell for any reason as personal representatives, there is no need for them to assent to themselves. They can quite simply sell as personal representatives under the authority of the grant.

Protection of purchasers

After 1925 a will is not abstracted and in a usual case the title will be:

1. conveyance to D;
2. death of D;
3. grant of representation;
4. assent to beneficiary.

If the beneficiary wishes to sell, a purchaser would wish to check that the beneficiary was actually entitled, ie that he did in fact inherit under the will. In order to avoid this necessity s36(7) AEA 1925 states that in favour of a purchaser an assent will be taken as sufficient evidence that the person in whose favour it is made is the person entitled to the legal estate, unless notice of a previous conveyance or assent is annexed to or indorsed on the grant.

The grant of probate or letters of administration relate to the whole estate of the deceased (with a few exceptions which it is not proposed to discuss here). When there is a sale or assent the original grant will be retained by the personal representatives, with a copy being handed over to complete the transferee's title. If there has been an assent or conveyance of land then this property no longer forms part of the estate, but the grant, on the face of it, could still include it. Thus, it is normal conveyancing practice, where there is an assent or conveyance, for a memorandum of that transaction to be indorsed on the grant which the personal representatives retain, so that if anyone in the future reads the grant they will see the memorandum and note that a particular asset is no longer included in the estate. A person taking an assent or a conveyance is entitled to have such an indorsement made: s36(5) AEA 1925. Where there is a death in a title, it is always part of the task of investigating title to ensure that appropriate memoranda have been indorsed on the grant.

Under this provision the assent is sufficient, not conclusive. Thus, in *Re Duce and Boots Cash Chemists (Southern) Ltd's Contract* [1937] Ch 642, the land was settled and the assent recited that fact, but the assent purported to vest the land in the beneficiary absolutely rather than as tenant for life under the Settled Land Act. It was held that the purchaser could object to the title provided as on the face of the assent it was incorrect since there should have been a vesting assent under the Settled Land Act.

A statement by a personal representative in a conveyance or assent that he has not made any previous assent or conveyance is sufficient evidence in favour of a purchaser that no previous assent or conveyance has been made, unless a memorandum of that previous disposition has been indorsed on the grant: s36(6) AEA 1925.

These provisions protect a purchaser, but not a beneficiary to whom property has been assented, as under s36(11) AEA 1925 a purchaser for these provisions is defined as a purchaser for money or money's worth.

Personal representatives have a statutory power of sale, and a purchaser does not have to investigate to ascertain the reason for the sale.

A conveyance by a personal representative is not invalidated by reason of the fact that the purchaser has notice of the fact that all debts, liabilities and legacies have been paid and there is therefore no need for a sale (s36(8) AEA 1925), and if a grant is revoked any conveyance to a purchaser made before the grant is revoked remains valid: s37 AEA 1925.

Registered land

The deceased will have been registered as proprietor. Personal representatives are entitled to be registered as proprietor in place of the deceased but normally they do not do so. A personal representative can assent or sell and the assentee or purchaser can then apply to the Land Registry to be registered as proprietor. The applicant will produce the land certificate, a copy of the grant and the assent or transfer and he will then be registered as proprietor. Any s36(6) statement in an assent would appear to be redundant, as once a purchaser is registered he has the legal title and any further dealing by the personal representative would not affect him. It should be noted that a person who acquires land under an assent is not a purchaser and is therefore bound by overriding interests, registered minor interests and any other minor interest subject to which the deceased held the land.

(It should also be remembered that under the Land Registration Act 1997, an assent of unregistered land now triggers compulsory first registration of title.)

9.5 Charities

The Charities Act 1993 contains provisions relating to transactions concerning land owned by charities which are a simplification of the previous rules under which the consent of the Charity Commissioners usually had to be obtained if a charity wished to sell land.

Under s36 a charity can grant a lease for under seven years without the consent of the Charity Commissioners if advice is taken from a suitably qualified person and the terms are the best which can be obtained.

Under this section the charity can also sell, lease or otherwise dispose of land without the consent of the Charity Commissioners provided certain requirements are fulfilled. The trustees must obtain a report from a suitably qualified person (normally a chartered surveyor) acting exclusively for the charity; they must consider and act on his report and advertise in accordance with his advice, and decide that in the light of the report the terms are the best which can be obtained. The conveyance, lease or transfer from the charity must contain a certificate confirming that these requirements have been complied with.

This relaxation does not apply if the transaction is with a connected person. This includes a trustee, a donor, a relative of either of these, an officer or employee of the charity or a spouse, or any company in which any of the above have a substantial interest. If the transaction is with a connected person, or the above requirements as to advice cannot be satisfied, then the consent of the Charity Commissioners or the court must be obtained to the transaction.

Under s38 a charity may mortgage land which it owns without the consent of the Charity Commissioners, if before completing the mortgage the charity trustees have taken independent advice from a suitably qualified person with no financial interest in the transaction on whether the transaction is necessary, whether the terms of the loan are reasonable and whether the charity is able to repay. Advice by an employee or officer of the charity can be acceptable for these purposes.

If a charity is the proprietor of registered land, then any restriction on the charity's ability to dispose of land will be contained in an appropriate restriction, and a purchaser will need to ensure that the terms of the restriction are complied with.

9.6 Persons under a disability

Minors

A minor cannot hold a legal estate in land either alone or jointly: s1(6) LPA. Under the 1925 legislation the effect of a transfer to a minor depended on the precise circumstances. A conveyance to a minor or minors jointly took effect as an agreement for valuable consideration to create a settlement in favour of the minor(s) and in the meantime to hold the property on trust for them. A conveyance to an adult and a minor jointly had the effect of transferring the legal estate to the adult to hold upon the statutory trusts.

This is changed by TOLATA: Sch 1 para 1. Now, if a person purports to convey land to a minor or minors, the conveyance is not effective to pass the legal estate but operates as a declaration that the land is held in trust for the minor(s). If land is conveyed to an adult or adults and a minor or minors, the conveyance vests the land in the adult(s) upon trust for the minor(s) and other person(s).

Where on commencement date, 1 January 1997, a conveyance was operating as a contract to create a settlement, then that agreement ceased to have effect and thereafter the conveyance operated as a declaration that the property was held in trust for the minors.

In any other circumstance where a legal estate would vest in a minor, the land will be held in trust for him.

In all these circumstances there will be a trust of land to which the appropriate provisions of TOLATA apply.

Mental illness

The effects of mental illness depend on whether or not a receiver under the Mental Health Act 1983 has been appointed.

If a receiver has not been appointed, a contract entered into by a mentally disordered person is valid unless the purchaser knew of the incapacity in which case it will be voidable. The position is similar if there is a sale by person with a mental incapacity or a purchase by him. A gift is however void.

If a receiver has been appointed because the patient is incapable of dealing with his own affairs, the patient loses all contractual capacity and his affairs come under the supervision of the Court of Protection. Any disposition by such a patient will be void. A receiver will be appointed to deal with the patient's affairs and subject to the approval of the Court the receiver will be able to deal with the patient's property.

When dealing with such a receiver, a purchaser needs to ensure that appropriate court orders authorising the transaction have been made and also needs to check the order appointing the receiver.

9.7 Attorneys

Introduction

A person (the donor of a power) can authorise the donee of the power (the attorney) to do any act which the donor can do. In particular, in conveyancing, a power of attorney authorises the attorney to execute deeds on the donor's behalf. Delegation by trustees raises particular problems: see Chapter 9, section 9.1.

When dealing with documents executed under a power of attorney two questions need to be addressed:

1. Was the power in existence when the attorney executed the deed?
2. Was the execution of the deed within the authority of the attorney?

Ordinary powers of attorney

These are regulated by the Powers of Attorney Act 1971.

Existence
A power of attorney can be given by any person of full age with mental capacity. A power of attorney can be revoked expressly by the donor, and is revoked automatically by the donor's death, bankruptcy or supervening mental incapacity. An exception to this is that a security power of attorney, ie one which is expressed to be irrevocable and which is given to secure some proprietary interest of the donee, cannot be revoked by the donor of the power as long as the donee has the interest without the donee's consent, although it will be revoked by the donor's death, bankruptcy or insanity: s4. An example of such a power could be in relation to an equitable mortgage, when the mortgagor gives the mortgagee a power of attorney to enable the mortgagee to transfer the fee simple in the event of default by the mortgagor. While the mortgage subsists, the power cannot be revoked by the mortgagor.

Protection of purchasers
There is a problem for persons dealing with an attorney since the validity of a transaction concluded by the attorney will depend on the power being in existence at the time the deed is executed, and it may unknown to him have been revoked. Section 5 affords a purchaser protection.

Where a power of attorney has been revoked and a person without knowledge of the revocation deals with the attorney, in his favour the transaction is as valid as if the power had not been revoked: s5(2). If the power is expressed to be irrevocable and given by way of security, then a person dealing with the attorney can assume that it can only be revoked with the consent of the donee and can ignore revocation by any other method, unless he knows that in fact the power was not given by way of security.

This section gives protection to a person dealing with the attorney; if that person does not know that the power has been revoked then the transaction with the attorney is valid. If that person subsequently wishes to sell, then he has to be in a position to establish to the satisfaction of a prospective purchaser that at the time he acquired the property he had no knowledge of revocation. In favour of such a subsequent purchaser it will be conclusively presumed that the person who dealt with the attorney had no knowledge of revocation:

1. if the transaction between that person and the attorney was completed within 12 months of the grant of the power;
2. if the transaction was completed more than 12 months from the grant of the power, if that person either at the time of completion of the transaction with the attorney or within three months makes a statutory declaration that he did not know of a revocation: s5(4).

Scope

In order to confirm that a transaction is authorised by the power of attorney, the power should be checked. It may in terms be limited to a particular transaction or transactions. A general power of attorney in the form set out in Sch 1 to the Act or in a similar form, in each case stating that the power is made in accordance with s10 of the Act, operates to confer on the attorney authority to do on behalf of the donor of the power anything which the donor could do himself.

Enduring powers of attorney

An ordinary power of attorney is automatically revoked by the mental incapacity of the donor of the power. It was recognised that this was inconvenient, in that the power ceased to have effect in many cases just when it would be most needed.

In 1985 the Enduring Powers of Attorney Act was passed, which enables a person to create a power of attorney which will not be revoked by mental incapacity – an enduring power of attorney. Such a power can either be a general power or a power limited to particular transactions. In order for a power to be an enduring power it has to be in the prescribed form. It contains a statement that it is intended to continue if the donor become mentally incapable. Until mental incapacity occurs it takes effect as an ordinary power of attorney.

When the donor of an enduring power becomes mentally incapable, unlike an ordinary power an enduring power is not revoked. As soon as the attorney has reason to believe that the donor is, or is becoming, mentally incapable he is then under a duty to apply for registration of the power with the Court of Protection. After the application for registration has been submitted, and while it is pending, the attorney has a limited power to act – he can take action to maintain the donor of the power or himself or other persons or to prevent loss to the donor's property. In the interim any transaction outside these limited matters can only be done if it is authorised by the court. Notice of disclaimer of the power by the attorney is ineffective unless notice is given to the court. If a receiver has been appointed under the Mental Health Act 1983 then the power cannot be registered. Once the power has been registered then the full powers conferred by the power again become exercisable. Once a power has been registered, it cannot be revoked by the donor during a lucid interval without the consent of the court, and notice of disclaimer by the attorney must be given to the court for the disclaimer to be effective.

The Enduring Powers of Attorney Act 1985 adopts the scheme for protection of purchasers which applies in relation to ordinary powers above by applying s5 of the 1971 Act.

Under s3(3) of the 1985 Act an enduring power of attorney could confer on the donee of the power all the donor's functions and powers as trustee. This provision was revoked by the Trustee Delegation Act 1999. An enduring power created after the commencement of that Act (1 March 2000) will not confer trustee powers. After the expiry of 12 months from that date, this provision will also apply to powers created before the Act came into force, unless an application for registration of the power has already been made.

For an enduring power of attorney to confer trustee functions on the attorney, the procedure under s1 Trustee Delegation Act 1999 (see section 9.1) must be followed

9.8 Voluntary dispositions

A gift will not normally be acceptable as a good root of title. Where there is a gift in the title it should be noted that on the occasion of a gift the title will probably not have been investigated, searches will not have been done and as a donee is not a purchaser he will take the property subject to equitable interests. It should also be noted that under the Land Registration Act 1997 a gift now triggers compulsory first registration.

A particular problem with gifts is the effect of insolvency legislation, because in some circumstances in insolvency a voluntary disposition of land may be set aside.

Under s339 of the Insolvency Act 1986 a transaction at an undervalue is voidable at the request of the trustee in bankruptcy. A transaction at an undervalue is defined as a gift, a transaction in consideration of marriage, or a transaction where the consideration received is of significantly less value than the consideration provided. Where there is a transaction at an undervalue and the transferor goes bankrupt, the trustee in bankruptcy can apply to the court to have the transaction set aside if the transfer was made within two years of the bankruptcy; this period is extended to five years if at the time of the transaction the transferor was insolvent or became insolvent as a result of the transaction. If the transaction at an undervalue occurred over five years before the bankruptcy, then there is no problem. In this context insolvency is defined as being unable to pay debts as they fall due, or where the value of assets is less than liabilities. On an application, the court can set aside the transaction and, inter alia, require any property transferred by the bankrupt to be vested in the trustee in bankruptcy, release or discharge any security provided by the bankrupt or require any person to pay a sum of money to the trustee. The effect of this provision is to make the owner of property which has been given away by a person who becomes bankrupt vulnerable, in that if the donor is declared bankrupt then he may be ordered to return the property transferred. Section 342(2) makes it plain that an order under s339 may affect the property of any person whether or not he is the person with whom the bankrupt entered into the transaction, and an order can therefore be made against a person who acquired property from the donee.

There is however protection for a purchaser in s342(2) Insolvency Act 1986, as amended by the Insolvency (No 2) Act 1994. This states that an order under s339 shall not affect any property which was acquired from a person other than the bankrupt which was acquired in good faith and for value. (The donee of property will always be vulnerable if the donee is declared bankrupt during the relevant period, and these provisions afford him no protection.) Section 342(2A) amplifies this. If a person acquires property from the donee, and at the time of that acquisition he had notice of the 'relevant surrounding circumstances' and the 'relevant proceedings', then it will be presumed that he was not in good faith unless the contrary is proved. The 'relevant surrounding circumstances' are that the transaction was at an undervalue, and the 'relevant proceedings' are a bankruptcy petition or a bankruptcy order against the donor. Thus, for a person not to be in good faith he must have notice of both the fact of the gift and the fact that bankruptcy proceedings are in train against the donor. As the deed of gift will be in the title deeds, a person dealing with the donee will have notice of the surrounding circumstances; in order to avoid notice of proceedings a bankruptcy search must be made against the donor prior to completion with the donee.

Take the following examples:

1. On 1 June 1993 A gave property to B.

   If A is declared bankrupt on 1 March 1995 the trustee can recover the property from B whether or not A was solvent at the time of the transfer.

   If A is declared bankrupt on 1 March 1998 the trustee can recover the property from B only if A was insolvent when he made the gift.

   If A is declared bankrupt on 1 March 1999 the trustee can make no claim against B.

2. On 1 June 1993 A gave property to B, and at the time of the gift he was

insolvent. On 1 December 1995 A is declared bankrupt. On 1 June 1996 B sold the property to C.

An order can be made against C unless he can claim the protection of the section. When he purchased from B in 1996 the title he saw would have included the conveyance to A and the deed of gift from A to B; he would therefore have had notice of the surrounding circumstances. In order to obtain protection he also has to have no notice of bankruptcy proceedings against A and he should therefore, prior to completion on 1 June 1996, have done a land charges search against A as bankruptcy proceedings are registrable and registration is notice. Provided he obtained a clear search stating no proceedings had been issued against A, C would be protected. If the search revealed the bankruptcy proceedings against A, then C would lose protection. Similarly, if bankruptcy proceedings had been registered against A and C did not do a search he would be deemed to have notice by virtue of the registration. In these latter two cases he would on the statutory definition not be in good faith and he would not therefore be protected.

The situation in relation to registered land is somewhat different. If there is a note on the register to the effect that there was a transaction at an undervalue within five years, then a purchaser will have notice and should make appropriate further enquiries. If there is no such note, then a purchaser can take the register at face value and will have no notice of the relevant surrounding circumstances.

10

The Purchase Deed

10.1 Introduction

10.2 Deeds – formalities

10.3 Conveyance

10.4 Transfer

10.1 Introduction

The purchase deed is normally drafted by the purchaser. In some cases, particularly where the seller is a developer who is selling plots on an estate, the seller will prepare the purchase deed to ensure that there is uniformity on matters such as easements and covenants.

Traditionally, the purchase deed has taken the form of a conveyance if the land is unregistered, and a transfer if the land is registered. There is an exception however in that under r72 LRR, where a sale of unregistered land will lead to first registration (which is now all sales) then a transfer rather than a conveyance can be used.

In preparing the purchase deed the purchaser will base it on the contract. The deed must contain all the relevant terms contained in the contract, as it is the purchase deed which will carry out the transaction contained in the contract. Nothing must be omitted, nor can anything which was not included in the contract be added.

10.2 Deeds – formalities

In order to convey or create a legal estate a deed is needed. It used to be necessary for a deed to be 'signed, sealed and delivered'. This is no longer the case, and the current rules relating to the execution of deeds are contained in s1 of the Law of Property (Miscellaneous Provisions) At 1989. For individuals the formalities are as follows. Under the 1989 Act it is no longer necessary for a deed to be sealed. To be a deed a document must make it clear on the face of it that it is a deed, and it must be validly executed. A deed is validly executed if it is signed by the person making the deed in the presence of a witness who attests the signature and it is delivered as a deed.

The formalities where a deed is to be executed by a corporation are set out in s74(1) LPA: the company seal has to be affixed in the presence of and be attested by the secretary and a director.

Delivery can be effected by physically handing over the deed; this is not necessary however and a deed will be delivered when the maker either by words or conduct shows an intention to be bound by it. Delivery can be either absolute – ie when it is of immediate effect – or conditional, in which case it is called an escrow. The seller will normally sign the deed some time before completion, and if the delivery were absolute at that time the purchaser would acquire the legal estate, even though the purchase price had not been paid. Delivery in escrow is conditional upon some event, usually the payment of the purchase price. Only when the condition is fulfilled will the deed come fully into effect and pass the legal estate. In a normal conveyancing transaction, therefore, even where a seller has signed the deed in advance of completion, it will be conditional on the price being paid and until it is paid the deed will be of no effect. Once an escrow is delivered it cannot be cancelled or withdrawn by the person delivering it pending fulfilment of the condition. This is important for a purchaser in a transaction where there is no contract but which is proceeding straight to completion.

Once the condition is fulfilled, then the deed takes effect without redelivery and the deed takes effect not at the date the condition is fulfilled but at the time of delivery in escrow. In *Hooper* v *Ramsbottom* (1815) 6 Taunt 12 the vendor executed an escrow conditional on the purchaser paying the purchase price. The vendor then executed an equitable mortgage by depositing the title deeds. The purchaser on offering the purchase price was entitled to the deeds and the conveyance and took the land free from the equitable mortgage. In *Alan Estates Ltd* v *WG Stores Ltd* [1982] Ch 511 a lease was delivered in escrow on 1 November 1976. The condition was fulfilled on 18 November 1997. The lease provided that rent was to be paid 'from the date hereof' but no date was ever inserted in the lease. It was held that rent was payable from 1 November 1976. Although the delivery relates back there are limits. It does not validate dealings by the purchaser with the land. The purchaser cannot, for example, collect the rents and profits, nor can he validly lease or mortgage. If he did purport to lease the land then the lease could be validated as soon as he acquired title by virtue of the feeding of the estoppel.

10.3 Conveyance

An example of the traditional form of conveyance used in unregistered land is contained in Appendix 4. The conveyance comprises the following elements:

1. *Date.* This will be the date of actual completion.
2. *The parties.* These will normally be the parties referred to in the contract.
3. *Recitals.* These begin with the word 'Whereas'. It is not necessary to have recitals, but the purpose is to record the basis of the agreement and possibly the factual background. Recitals can serve various useful evidential purposes.

   Under s45(6) LPA recitals of facts in a deed over 20 years old shall, unless the contrary is proved, be taken as sufficient evidence of the truth of those facts.

   Under s38 Trustee Act 1925 a statement in a document appointing a new trustee to the effect that the new appointment is justified on one of the grounds in s36 – eg, a trustee is out of the United Kingdom, refuses to act or is incapable of acting – is in favour of a purchaser of the legal estate conclusive evidence of the matter stated, and in favour of a purchaser any appointment of a trustee depending on that statement is valid.

   There is also the principle of estoppel by deed. Under this principle, a recital in a deed may operate as an estoppel against the person making it so that he cannot subsequently deny the truth of it.
4. *Consideration.* A statement of the consideration is confirmation of the fact that this is not a voluntary disposition, and is the basis on which stamp duty will be paid.
5. *Receipt clause.* A purchaser would normally wish to ensure that the seller receives the purchase money. In a routine conveyancing transaction the purchase money is handed to the seller's solicitor not the seller personally. Under s69 LPA, where the deed contains a receipt clause, this is sufficient authority for the purchaser to pay the money to the seller's solicitor without requiring any other form of authority.
6. *Covenants for title.* The basic common law principle is that on completion the contract merged in the conveyance and no proceedings could be taken under the contract. In order to give the purchaser protection after completion, it became the practice to include in a conveyance certain covenants for title which remained in force after completion.

   Section 76 LPA implied certain covenants into conveyances. The full covenants were set out in Sch 2. In summary, if a person conveyed as and was expressed to convey as beneficial owner there were implied the following covenants:

   a) A covenant that the seller had a good right to convey. If the land were conveyed subject to an undisclosed incumbrance then this covenant would be broken.
   b) A covenant for quiet enjoyment. This was a covenant that the purchaser would not be disturbed in his enjoyment of the property purchased, and included a covenant of indemnity by the seller if he was.
   c) A covenant that the property was free from incumbrances except those subject to which the property was sold.

d) A covenant for further assurance. This imposed an obligation on the seller to do any further act which was necessary to vest the property in the purchaser.

If the seller conveyed and was expressed to convey as trustee, mortgagee or personal representative there was implied only a covenant that he himself had not incumbered the property.

If the seller conveyed as and was expressed to convey as settlor, there was implied only a covenant for further assurance.

In a conveyance, therefore, the use of a specific expression imported lengthy covenants. For example, if in a conveyance the following form was used:

'A as beneficial owner hereby conveys to B ...'

then the four covenants specified above would be implied into the conveyance.

Section 76 uses the expressions 'conveys as ... and is expressed to convey as'. It used to be thought that these implied covenants were merely a form of shorthand which avoided setting out the lengthy covenants in full and if, for example the words used were 'beneficial owner' then the above covenants would be implied. However, the courts interpreted these provisions as not a simple word-saving exercise and required not only that a person should be expressed to convey as beneficial owner or trustee for example but should actually have that capacity in order for the covenants to be implied.

The Law Commission in 1991 recommended reform and the result was the Law of Property (Miscellaneous Provisions) Act 1994, which repealed s76 and replaced it with a new set of implied covenants for title.

Instead of using expressions such as beneficial owner or trustee, the Act introduced the new concepts of full and limited title guarantee.

Where a seller sells with full title guarantee, then the following covenants are implied:

a) That he has the right to dispose of the property as he purports to do: s2(1)(a).
b) That he will at his own cost do all that he reasonably can to give to the purchaser the title he is purporting to give: s2(1)(b). This includes in relation to registered land doing everything he reasonably can to ensure that the purchaser is registered with the title the seller had, and if the title to the land is to be registered, giving all reasonable assistance to establish to the satisfaction of the Land Registrar the right of the purchaser to be registered as proprietor: s2(2).
c) That the property is being transferred free from charges and incumbrances and other rights exercisable by third parties except those which he did not know of nor could reasonably be expected to know of: s3(1).

Under s6, however, these covenants do not extend to matters subject to which the transfer is expressly made, nor do they extend to matters which are within the actual knowledge of the purchaser.

Where the seller sells with limited title guarantee, the covenants under s2(1)(a) and (b) are also implied. The covenant under s3(1) is not implied where there is limited title guarantee. Where there is limited title guarantee, then there is a much more restricted covenant in s3(3), namely, that since the last disposition for value, the seller has not charged or incumbered the property or granted third party rights, or suffered the property to be so charged or incumbered and he is not aware that anyone else has done so.

Again, under s6, this covenant does not extend to matters subject to which the transaction expressly is to take effect or which are within the purchaser's actual knowledge.

Under s7 the benefit of these covenants is annexed to the estate or interest of the person to whom the disposition is made, and the covenants can be enforced by any person who acquires that estate or interest.

7. *Parcels.* This is the physical description of the land and should reflect the contract. See Chapter 4, section 4.2 for a detailed discussion on this.

Under s62 LPA a conveyance of land includes all those rights enjoyed with the land such as easements without express mention.

8. *Exceptions and reservations.* If there is a sale of part, the seller if he wishes to retain easements over the land sold must make express provision in the conveyance.

9. *Covenants.* If covenants are to be imposed then they must be expressly included.

10. *Beneficial ownership.* If there are two or more purchasers the beneficial entitlement can be dealt with in the conveyance. If the equitable interests are complicated then the better course of action is to deal with these in a separate trust deed as in this way the equitable interests are kept off the legal title.

11. *Acknowledgement and undertaking.* It may be that the purchaser will not on completion receive all the deeds and documents relating to the land being purchased. For example, the deeds may relate to land retained by the seller, or one of the documents may be a grant of probate or letters of administration which will be kept by the personal representatives and on completion a certified copy only will be handed over. In such a case an acknowledgement for production will be included. The effect of this is that if at any time in the future the purchaser needs to have sight of the original, then the seller must produce it. This may also be coupled with an undertaking for the safe custody of the specified documents.

12. *Certificate of value.* This is included to determine the amount of stamp duty. If the transaction is for value, then stamp duty will be paid at the appropriate rate on the consideration – under £60,000 exempt, between £60,000 and £250,000 at 1 per cent, between £250,000 and £500,000 at 3 per cent and over £500,000 at 4 per cent. If a certificate cannot be given for some reason then the document should be submitted to the Stamp Office for adjudication, a process whereby the Stamp Office will determine the amount of stamp duty payable. If the document is exempt from stamp duty under the Stamp Duty (Exempt Instruments)

Regulations 1987, eg a gift or transfer between spouses, then a certificate to the effect that the document comes within the appropriate category must be included.

13. *Execution.* As this is a deed it will have to be executed by the seller. There is no need for it to be executed by the purchaser unless he is undertaking obligations. It is necessary for purchasers to execute – for example, if there are two or more purchasers and the beneficial entitlement is dealt with, or if the purchaser is entering into new covenants. It is normal for purchasers to execute however, to confirm that they will be bound by the terms of the deed.

10.4 Transfer

This is much simpler and is in Form TR1 which is prescribed by the LRR. A copy is set out in Appendix 5.

1. *Stamp duty.* Here will be impressed the stamp duty payable after completion. There is a standard form of certificate of value which has to be completed in the appropriate way as the stamp duty position is the same for a transfer as for a conveyance.
2. *Title number.* This is the title number of the property. If this is a transfer under r72 there will be no title number.
3. *Property.* This is a description of the property, which will refer to the contract. If a transfer is being used under r72 (first registration), the description should refer to the last document of title which contains a description of the property.
4. *Date.* This will be the date of completion.
5., 6. and 7. *Transferor's* and *transferee's* names and addresses and transferee's address for service for entry on the register.
8. A simple statement that the *transferor transfers the property to the transferee.*
9. *Consideration.* The appropriate box should be completed and the wording incorporates a receipt clause with the same effect as in relation to a conveyance (above).
10. The relevant box is completed to indicate the title guarantee given.
11. *Declaration of trust.* This deals with the beneficial entitlement. Unless the transferees will hold as beneficial joint tenants, an appropriate restriction will be entered on the register in due course.
12. *Additional provisions.* Here are included any other clauses, such as the imposition of new covenants.
13. As the transfer is a deed the relevant execution formalities need to be followed.

11

Completion

11.1 Introduction

This is the date when the transaction contained in the contract will be carried out.

The purchaser prepares the purchase deed, executes it and forwards it to the seller for him to hold in readiness for completion. The seller will then execute it prior to completion.

The buyer has to carry out pre-completion searches. What searches have to be carried out will depend on whether the land is registered or unregistered.

11.2 Unregistered land

The buyer will have to carry out a search at the Land Charges Registry under the LCA. Under this Act land charges are registered against the name of the estate owner whose estate is to be affected: s3(1). Registration constitutes notice. A search will be made against the seller, and if there are any previous estate owners against whom there is not a search certificate in the epitome or abstract, and in respect of whom a search has not already been done, then a search needs to be done against those persons as well. The search is done by sending the relevant form to the Land Charges Registry. This will specify the name of the estate owner, the county and the time period. It will only be when a person owns a legal estate that a charge affecting the land can be registered and affect the land. It is therefore only necessary to search in relation to the period when a person actually owned the land. If this cannot be established then a search should be done since 1926. That was when the Land Charges Registry came into existence and by definition a search against the name from that date must reveal any adverse entries. The result of the search in the form of an official certificate is conclusive evidence in favour of a purchaser. If a charge is registered, but is not disclosed in the search, the purchaser takes free of it. It is important that any search is done against the correct name, since a search carried out against the wrong name will afford no protection to the purchaser and he will be bound by any entries which are registered even though the search does not reveal them. Equally, a charge registered in an incorrect name will not bind a purchaser who searches against the correct name. For example, in *Diligent Finance Co Ltd* v *Alleyne* (1972) 23 P & CR 346, a wife registered a Class F land charge against her husband in the name of Erskine Alleyne. A prospective mortgagee searched against Erskine Owen Alleyne which was the name in the deeds and the search did not reveal the entry. The mortgagee took free of the wife's interest.

Under the LCA the following are the most important matters which have to be registered:

1. Class B – charge imposed by statute, eg a charge for unpaid legal aid contributions.
2. Class C(i) – puisne mortgage, ie legal mortgage not protected by deposit of title deeds.
3. C(ii) – equitable mortgage not protected by deposit of title deeds.
4. C(iii) – general equitable charge, eg seller's lien for unpaid purchase price.
5. C(iv) – estate contract.
6. Class D (i) – Inland Revenue charge to secure unpaid inheritance tax.
7. Class D (ii) – post–1925 restrictive covenant.
8. Class D(iii) – equitable easement.
9. Class F – spouse's right of occupation.

In addition, legal actions involving land may appear in the register of pending actions (eg applications for ancillary relief in divorce, boundary disputes, claims based on adverse possession), and orders and judgements affecting land, may appear in the register of writs and orders affecting land. Bankruptcy petitions are registered in the register of pending actions, and bankruptcy orders are registered in the register of writs and orders.

A land charge of Class B and C(i), C(ii) and C(iii) and F is void against a purchaser of the land or any interest in it unless the charge is registered before completion

A land charge of Class C(iv) or D(i), D(ii) or D(iii) is void against a purchaser for money or money's worth of a legal estate in the land unless the charge is registered before completion of the purchase.

A pending action or writ or order is void against a purchaser in good faith of a legal estate for money or money's worth.

Section 198(1) LPA lays down the basic principle that a purchaser is not bound by an unregistered land charge of which he has notice.

In *Midland Bank Trust Co Ltd* v *Green* [1981] AC 513 the House of Lords emphasised that notice is irrelevant. In that case a father granted his son an option to purchase a farm. The father and son fell out and the father sold the farm to his wife for £500 when it was worth £40,000. The option was not registered and the issue was whether the wife was bound by it. It was held that the only thing which mattered was registration. As the option was not protected by registration the wife was not bound by it. It did not matter that the wife knew of the option, and there was no requirement that she should act in good faith. The House of Lords did not import the definition of purchaser in s205 LPA – in good faith and for valuable consideration – into this provision. The LCA states that unless the context otherwise requires, a purchaser is a person who takes an interest in land for valuable consideration. There is a requirement that a purchaser acts in good faith in relation to pending actions and writs and orders, but there is no such requirement in relation to land charges generally.

If a solicitor is acting for a mortgagee a bankruptcy search against the mortgagor must also be done: see Chapter 15, section 15.2 for further discussion of this.

Under the LCA a purchaser will be bound by a land charge which is registered at the time of completion. The search will obviously have to be done in anticipation of completion and therefore there could be a risk that a charge could be registered after the date of the search but before completion. In order to protect a purchaser in such a situation, an official search certificate from the Land Charges Registry confers a priority period of 15 working days. Where an official search certificate has been issued, a purchaser is not affected by any entry made on the register after the date of the certificate if completion takes place within 15 working days. In other words, in the purchaser's favour the register is frozen for the priority period. The priority period cannot be extended and if completion does not take place a new search certificate will be obtained which will contain any new registrations. For example, an official search has been made revealing no subsisting entries, with a priority period expiring on 30 June. On 20 June a Class F land charge is registered by the seller's spouse. If completion takes place before 30 June, the purchaser is not affected by the Class F land charge. If, however, completion does not take place within the priority period, a new search will have to be made. If this is done on 29 June, this will reveal the Class F land charge which will affect the purchaser. It is not possible for the original priority period to be extended so as to prolong the protection afforded to the purchaser by the original search.

The only exception to this is that if it is intended to register a land charge which is to be created on completion, a priority notice can be registered. In such a case, if the application for registration is made within 30 days of the registration of the priority notice, the registration relates back to the date when the charge was created.

11.3 Registered land

Where the title to land is registered, it is the state of the register which is relevant for a purchaser. The purchaser will have been provided with office copy entries as part of the documentation and they will disclose the state of the register at the date of the entries. Alternatively, the charge or land certificate will specify a date when the certificate was compared with the register. The purchaser wishes to ensure that no changes have been made to the register since the date of the office copy entries or the date the entries were compared.

This search is done by completing a form requiring the Land Registry to confirm whether any adverse entry has been made since the appropriate date. The result is in the form of a certificate confirming either that no entries have been made, or, if they have, giving details. As with unregistered land, a purchaser needs protection against last minute registration of matters. In registered land this is also achieved by conferring a priority period on the result of the search. Once the search certificate has been issued, the purchaser is not affected by any matters subsequently registered, provided that he completes and applies for the transaction to be registered within 30 working days. It should be noted that within this priority period the transaction must be completed and an application for registration lodged, whereas the priority period in relation to a Land Charges Registry search relates only to completion. Again, the priority period cannot be extended: see, eg, *Watts* v *Waller* [1973] QB 153. In this case X had contracted to sell his house to Y. Y obtained an official certificate of search, with priority ending on 25 May. After the search, on 10 May X's wife applied for the entry of a notice under the Matrimonial Homes Act 1983 to protect her right of occupation. Completion took place on 24 May, but Y only applied for registration after the expiry of the priority period. The result was that Y took subject to X's wife's rights.

Unlike a land charges search, the Land Registry search is not conclusive in favour of a purchaser, but if it is wrong a purchaser can claim compensation from the Chief Land Registrar.

11.4 Company search

If land is unregistered, if the seller is a company it will be necessary to carry out a search of the register at Companies House. This may have been done at the pre-contract stage. If it has been then it should be redone just before completion. As a company search confers no priority it should be done only very shortly before completion. Prior to 1970 a mortgage created by a company could be protected by registration at Companies House under the Companies Acts. Since 1970 that is not possible, and any mortgage must be protected where appropriate in the Land Charges Register. It will be necessary to check in the Companies Register for pre-1970 charges. Also, floating charges are registered at Companies House and not in the Land Charges Registry. If a floating charge is revealed, then a letter of non-crystallisation will be needed. (A floating charge is a charge created by a company over its assets, which 'floats' over the assets and which permits the company to deal with its assets until the charge crystallises. A charge crystallises when a specified event occurs which makes the sums secured by the charge payable, eg default in payment or appointment of a receiver. When the charge crystallises it becomes a fixed charge attached to the assets and the company is no longer able to deal with them.) A company search will also confirm that the company is in existence, has not been struck off and is not in liquidation.

Although in registered land the register is conclusive, it is normal to do a companies search in order to check that there are no winding-up proceedings and that there are no floating charges which do not have to be registered at the Land Registry.

11.5 Completion

The purchaser has to check that the title deeds which he receives are in accordance with the evidence of title which has been given by the seller, as this will normally be the first time that the purchaser actually sees the original title deeds. The seller hands over the deeds in return for the purchase price.

In unregistered land, the purchaser checks the title deeds; if he does not receive the originals because, for example, they relate to land retained by the seller, then he needs to ensure that the copies are certified as true copies and appropriate memoranda of the sale endorsed on the deeds which the seller retains. The purchaser will receive the title deeds, including the conveyance to him. On completion the legal estate vests in the purchaser.

In registered land, the seller hands over the land or charge certificate, any other necessary documents, such as evidence of discharge of mortgages, and the transfer. On completion the legal estate does not vest in the purchaser; the legal estate does not vest until the purchaser is registered as proprietor.

In addition to the title deeds, there will also be handed over any other relevant documents such as guarantees. In particular, on completion the issue of NHBC cover needs to be considered. Under this scheme where there is a new property, the NHBC (National House Builders' Council) issue insurance cover. There is a certificate requiring the developer to remedy faults occurring within the first two years and after that until ten years have elapsed there is insurance cover for major defects. If the purchaser is the first purchaser of a new property, then it has to be ensured that the NHBC cover is in force on completion; if the house is being sold within ten years of construction then the relevant documentation needs to be handed over to the purchaser.

11.6 Merger

On completion the contract is said to merge in the conveyance so that no action can be brought on the contract – hence the development of the covenants for title: see Chapter 10, section 10.3. However, a provision for vacant possession does not merge (*Hissett* v *Reading Roofing Co Ltd* [1969] 1 WLR 1757), nor does an express provision for compensation for misdescription: *Palmer* v *Johnson* (1884) 13 QBD 351.

Also, there will be no merger if there is a contrary provision in the contract. When the Standard Conditions are used there will be such a provision: SC 7.4.

11.7 Post-completion work

Unless the conveyance is exempt then stamp duty will have to be paid by the purchaser. And, even if no duty is payable, details of the transaction have to be supplied to the Inland Revenue.

If the land is unregistered, the purchaser will have to apply for first registration of title. If the title is already registered, the purchaser will have to apply for the registration of the dealing – bearing in mind any priority period applicable to a search. The general principle is that any registrable dealing must be registered and until this is done no legal interest is conferred on the purchaser. Thus, the following must be registered to give the purchaser a legal interest: a transfer, a mortgage or charge, the grant of an easement or the grant of a lease of over 21 years.

12

Late Completion

12.1 Introduction

12.2 Completion notice

12.3 Interest for late completion

12.1 Introduction

Completion date is normally not of the essence and therefore a failure to complete on the contractual date by one party does not end the contract, nor entitle the party not in default to treat the contract as ended. However, this does not mean that the party not in default is without a remedy – the defaulting party is in breach of contract.

12.2 Completion notice

Under an open contract a person who is ready and able to complete may, after a reasonable time, serve a completion notice specifying a date for completion which must be after a reasonable period and the new date for completion is of the essence. This is too vague to be satisfactory and accordingly the Standard Conditions contain detailed provisions which override the open contract position.

Standard Condition 6.8 deals with this.

> 'SC 6.8.1 At any time on or after completion date, a party who is ready able and willing to complete may give the other a notice to complete.
> 6.8.3 The parties are to complete the contract within ten working days of giving a notice to complete, excluding the day on which the notice is given. For this purpose time is of the essence of the contract.
> 6.8.4 On receipt of a notice to complete:
> a) if a buyer has paid no deposit, he is forthwith to pay a deposit of ten per cent
> b) if the buyer paid a deposit of less than ten per cent, he is forthwith to pay a further deposit equal to the balance of that ten per cent.'

It will be seen that it is a prerequisite to the service of a notice to complete that the party giving the notice must be ready able and willing to complete. Thus, for example, a vendor who has not answered requisitions would not be able to serve a completion notice.

Standard Condition 6.8.2 defines ready able and willing to complete as follows:

'A party is ready able and willing:
a) if he could be but for the default of the other party, and
b) in the case of the seller, even though a mortgage remains secured on the property, if the amount to be paid on completion enables the property to be transferred freed of all mortgages (except those to which the sale is subject).'

Standard Condition 6.8.2(b) avoids the consequences of *Cole* v *Rose* [1973] 3 All ER 1121. In that case it was decided that a vendor was not able to complete if the property was subject to an undischarged mortgage and the seller's solicitor had not given an undertaking to discharge it on completion.

Once the completion notice has been served, time becomes of the essence for both parties. For example, a seller may serve a notice to complete, but if he then fails to complete a purchaser may treat the contract as discharged and does not have to serve his own completion notice: *Finkielkrant* v *Monohan* [1949]] 2 All ER 234.

The existence of the Standard Conditions does not deprive a party of his rights under the general law. For example, if the innocent party serves a notice which is bad (eg served on one only of joint parties), the innocent party can still rely on the rule that he can treat the contract as discharged by unreasonable delay: *Woods* v *Mackenzie Hill Ltd* [1975] 2 All ER 170.

In *Dimsdale Developments (South East) Ltd* v *De Haan* (1984) 47 P & CR 1 there was a contract by reference to the National Conditions (a precursor of the Standard Conditions). Under those conditions there was an express saving for other rights and remedies. The seller served a notice to complete and there was doubt as to whether the correct contractual notice had been given. The court considered that even if the completion notice did not comply with the specific contractual requirements, it could be a valid notice under the open contract rules, ie it could be effective provided it gave a reasonable length of time.

If a vendor serves an invalid completion notice, and in reliance on it subsequently states that the contract is terminated, that is a wrongful repudiation of the contract which the purchaser can accept and claim damages: *Rightside Properties Ltd* v *Gray* [1975] Ch 72.

If completion takes place after service of a notice to complete, the innocent party can either claim damages or interest under the contract.

Failure to comply

Once a notice to complete has been served it binds both parties.

If the buyer fails to complete following the service of a completion notice, the position is regulated by SC 7.5 as follows:

'SC 7.5.2 The seller may rescind the contract and if he does so:
a) he may
i) forfeit and keep any deposit and accrued interest
ii) resell the property

iii) claim damages
b) the buyer is to return any documents he received from the seller and is to cancel any registration of the contract.'

Under SC 7.5.3 the seller retains all other rights and remedies.

If the seller fails to complete in accordance with a completion notice, the position is regulated by SC 7.6:

'SC 7.6.2 The buyer may rescind the contract, and if he does so:
a) the deposit is to be repaid to the buyer with accrued interest
b) the buyer is to return any documents he received from the seller and is, at the seller's expense, to cancel any registration of the contract.'

Under SC 7.6.3 the buyer retains other rights and remedies.

It will be noted from these provisions that failure by one party to comply with a notice to complete does not discharge the contract automatically but enables the non-defaulting party to treat the contract as discharged if he so wishes. (In this context 'rescind' means that the non-defaulting party may treat the contract as discharged, but retains his other contractual remedies.) Instead of treating the contract as discharged, the non-defaulting party can substitute a new date for that under the original completion notice, which new date will be the contractual date in relation to which time will again be of the essence. This procedure, of substituting a new date should be distinguished from waiver. If after a notice to complete has expired the parties continue to negotiate for completion, in circumstances which indicate that the parties regard the contract as still subsisting, then time will no longer be treated as of the essence on the basis that it has been waived by the non-defaulting party. If time is to be of the essence in relation to completion, then a further completion notice would have to be served.

12.3 Interest for late completion

Under SC 7.3 provision is made for the payment of interest if completion is delayed through the fault of one party. Compensation is calculated at the contract rate and accrues on a daily basis. If the seller is in default, compensation is calculated at the contract rate on the purchase price for the period for which he is in default. If the buyer is in default compensation is calculated on the purchase price less any deposit paid. If both parties are in default, the party whose default is the greater has to pay compensation calculated by reference to the period by which his default exceeds the default of the other, or the period between the contractual completion date and actual completion if that is shorter.

13

Remedies

13.1 Introduction

Most conveyancing transactions proceed to a satisfactory conclusion. If there is delay in completion then the position of the parties is as set out in Chapter 12. However, there will be cases where matters are not brought to a conclusion or where the remedies outlined there are insufficient. It should be borne in mind that the remedies available are essentially an application of general contract law and reference should be made to contract books for more detailed general information

The following situations can be identified:

1. where one party does not complete;
2. where one party wishes to set up a breach by the other to justify a failure to complete;
3. where completion takes place but there are outstanding matters to be resolved.

Consideration will first be given to the contractual position and then reference will be made to misrepresentation.

13.2 Specific performance

It may be the case that a completion notice has been served but has not been complied with. The non-defaulting party may then consider applying for an order of specific performance.

This is an equitable remedy which, as with all such remedies, is discretionary. It will only be granted as a contractual remedy where damages are inadequate. It has always been said that contracts for the sale of land are unique in that each piece of land is unique and therefore damages for breach will not be adequate. In practice, in most cases a seller will be content to rely on his usual contractual remedies if the buyer does not complete – forfeit the deposit, resell and, if appropriate, claim damages, especially if the failure to complete is the result of inability to proceed as specific performance would not achieve anything. If specific performance is ordered, then the claimant's contractual rights under the provisions relating to completion notices cease as the contractual rights are superseded by the terms of the court order. A party claiming specific performance must show that there is a valid, enforceable contract which is sufficiently certain to be the subject of specific performance. He must also be ready and willing to complete. General contractual defences, such as mistake, will be available as defences to specific performance, but there are also other matters which will operate as a bar. As this is an equitable remedy the person claiming it must 'come with clean hands'.

Delay

The Limitation Acts do not apply to equitable remedies. These are subject to the doctrine of laches, whereby unreasonable delay will be a bar to equitable relief. This period may well be shorter than the similar limitation period, especially if the defendant has acted to his detriment and would be prejudiced if specific performance were ordered.

Defective title

Specific performance will not be ordered if the effect would be to make the purchaser accept a bad or doubtful title.

Third party rights

Specific performance will not be ordered if third parties have obtained rights in the property. Thus, for example, if a seller has not completed, specific performance will not be ordered if he has transferred the property to a third party in the interim.

Hardship

If the order of specific performance would cause hardship to the defendant then it may be refused.

Damages adequate

If in all the circumstances damages would be an adequate compensation, then specific performance will not be granted.

Damages in lieu

Under s50 Supreme Court Act 1981 the court can, where it could have awarded specific performance, award damages in lieu. This power is only available if specific performance could have been granted but, for example, because of hardship it is not. The power to award damages does not exist if for some reason specific performance could not have been ordered at all. In *Biggin* v *Minton* [1977] 1 WLR 701 it was held that this power to award damages exists not only initially but also where specific performance has been initially ordered but has turned out to be unworkable. In *Johnson* v *Agnew* [1980] AC 367 it was held that where an order for specific performance had not been complied with, the non-defaulting party could treat that as a repudiation by the other party, have the order for specific performance discharged and claim common law damages. In *Wroth* v *Tyler* [1974] Ch 30 the issue of computation was discussed. In that case the contract price of a property was £6,000, by completion date (the date of breach) the value had risen to £7,700, and at the date of the judgment the value was £11,500. The court refused specific performance and awarded damages based on the value at the date specific performance was refused, as damages were in lieu of the specific performance which would otherwise have been ordered.

13.3 Damages

General

Damages may be claimed either where there is no completion or where there is completion but there is some breach including delay. Where there is delay, an innocent party is entitled to claim compensation under SC 7.5 or SC 7.6: see Chapter 12. If this is not sufficient, then he can pursue a claim for damages. It may be that a non-defaulting party who could treat the contract as discharged by the breach wishes to complete, or that the breach is not of such magnitude as to permit the non-defaulting party to treat the contract as discharged. Any claim for damages for breach of contract must be brought within six years of the breach unless the contract was in a deed, in which case the limitation period is 12 years. Damages are assessed under the general contractual principles laid down in *Hadley* v *Baxendale* (1854) 9 Exch 341. Damages in contract will compensate a party for:

1. loss arising naturally from the breach;

2. loss that does not arise naturally from the breach but which is within the contemplation of the parties at the time of the contract.

In any claim for damages, credit will have to be given for any deposit forfeited or any compensation paid under SC 7.5 or 7.6, and any person claiming damages will be under the general duty to mitigate his loss.

Seller

If the transaction is not completed then the seller has remedies under SC 7.5 – in particular, he may forfeit the deposit and resell. He may do this even if he has not suffered any loss. If he wishes to pursue a claim for damages, then the basic measure of damages will be for loss of bargain – the difference between the contract price and the value of the land. He will not be able to claim wasted expenses in addition, as if the transaction had been completed these would have been deducted from the proceeds of sale. A seller could, however, claim wasted expenses instead of loss of bargain.

Buyer

If the seller is in default the buyer is entitled to the return of his deposit and again loss of bargain – the difference between the contract price and the value of the property. He has his money but in theory he has to buy an alternative similar property. Again he cannot claim his expenses as these would be paid in any event if the matter had proceeded, nor can he recover expenses not actually incurred. These items come under the first limb in *Hadley* v *Baxendale* – loss arising naturally from the breach. Other matters of loss, such as loss of profit on development or a subsale, come within the second limb, and whether a buyer can recover these depends on whether the seller knew of the buyer's plans. For example, in *Cottrill* v *Steyning and Littlehampton Building Society* [1966] 1 WLR 753 the seller knew of the buyer's plans to develop the land which he was buying. The damages assessed took into account the profits which both parties were aware would be made by the purchaser following completion.

Date of assessment

The general common law principle is that damages are assessed at the date of the breach of contract. This may result in injustice if, for example, property prices are increasing. In *Johnson* v *Agnew* [1980] AC 367 the House of Lords stated that this was not an immutable rule, in that the court could fix some other date which would avoid injustice, such as the date of the hearing. The court stated that there was no difference in approach to assessing equitable damages in lieu of specific performance and common law damages, and the basis of assessment is now the same.

The rule in **Bain** *v* **Fothergill** *(1874) LR 7 HL 58*

This case laid down the principle that where a seller was unable to perform the contract because of a defect in his title, the damages a purchaser could claim were limited to the return of the deposit and interest and reimbursement of his conveyancing costs – there was no entitlement to damages for loss of bargain. This rule was abolished in relation to contracts made after 27 September 1989 by s3 Law of Property (Miscellaneous Provisions) Act 1989.

13.4 Discharge

It may be that a party will allege that a breach by the other entitles him to treat the contract as discharged and justifies a failure to complete. This could be raised, for example, as a defence to an action for damages or a claim for specific performance, or it could be raised independently. Not all breaches of contract enable an innocent party to treat the contract as discharged. Some minor breaches do not allow this but merely give rise to a claim for damages. One example of a breach which gives an innocent party the right to treat the contract as terminated which has been examined is a failure to comply with a notice to complete. A party may decide not to treat the contract as discharged even if entitled to do so, but may choose to continue to perform it and claim damages. Whether a party is entitled to treat the contract as discharged depends on whether the breach goes to the root of the contract – an essential term – or is a breach of a non-essential term. Only in the case of the former will breach entitle an innocent party to treat the contract as discharged. If the seller treats the contract as discharged he may forfeit the deposit and claim damages. If the purchaser treats the contract as discharged he is entitled to the return of the deposit and may claim damages. If he has been let into possession he obviously has to vacate. Apart from claims for damages the contract is at an end and, for example, specific performance is not available since that depends on the existence of an enforceable contract.

13.5 Restrictions on remedies

Standard Conditions 7.1 and 7.2 define the rights of the parties where there has been an error or omission in the contract.

Under SC 7.1.2, if there is a misleading plan or statement in a contract due to an error or omission, the injured party is entitled to damages if there is a material difference between the description or value of the property as represented and as it is.

Under SC 7.1.3 such an error or omission only entitles a party to treat the contract as discharged if the error or omission is the result of fraud or recklessness, or if the innocent party would have to his prejudice to accept or transfer property differing substantially (in quality, quantity or tenure) from that which he had been led to expect.

Thus neither party will be entitled to damages if there is a trivial mistake, and SC 7.1.3 lays down when a party can treat a contract as discharged.

13.6 Other remedies

If the contract as drawn does not accurately reflect the agreement between the parties then it may possible to apply to the court for rectification.

Under s49(2) LPA, the court has a general power to order the return of a deposit.

13.7 After completion

The open contract position is that the contract merges on completion, and after completion no action can be taken on the contract. This does not apply under the Standard Conditions, as there is a declaration of non-merger contained in SC 7.4. After completion, the purchaser will have the benefit of the covenants for title which were given in the transfer and can claim in respect of a breach: see Chapter 10, section 10.3. Remedies for misrepresentation continue after completion.

Under s25 LPA 1969 a purchaser of unregistered land may in some circumstances be able to claim compensation from the Chief Land Registrar if the land is affected by a registered land charge of which he had no notice.

The purchaser can claim compensation if he suffers loss because:

1. he is affected by a registered land charge;
2. the charge is registered against an estate owner who does not appear as such in the abstract of title;
3. at completion the purchaser had no actual knowledge of the land charge.

He cannot claim if the land charge is referred to in a document which is in the abstract, and if the purchaser agrees to accept less than 15 years title he cannot claim compensation if an investigation of the title from a root at least 15 years old would have revealed the land charge.

13.8 Misrepresentation

Introduction

An incorrect statement made before the contract is concluded by the seller or his agent may be a misrepresentation and give the buyer remedies. It will invariably be the seller who makes a representation but, in theory a buyer could also be liable for misrepresentation. It does not matter that the misrepresentation has become a term of the contract and the remedies for misrepresentation remain available after completion. Misrepresentations may occur when preliminary inquiries are being answered or during pre-contract negotiations, and care therefore needs to be taken in precisely how answers are given.

Essentials

A misrepresentation is an untrue statement of fact made by one contracting party to the other on which the other party relies, which operates as an inducement to him to enter the contract and as a result of which he suffers loss.

The statement must first be incorrect. It must also be a statement of fact not a statement of opinion, although it may be difficult in some cases to distinguish. A misrepresentation may not be verbal, eg a seller may cover up cracks or paint rotten timber. A statement that an opinion is held is itself a statement of fact, and so if a seller states that he is not aware of a defect when he is, that is a statement of fact.

The statement must be an inducement; if it is material and is relevant inducement will easily be found. There can, however, be no inducement if the purchaser knows that the statement is incorrect. In *Strover* v *Harrington* [1988] Ch 390 there was an incorrect statement in the agents' particulars and in replies to preliminary inquiries that the property had mains drainage. The agents realised the mistake and informed the buyers' solicitors but the buyers themselves were not told. They failed in misrepresentation as they had imputed knowledge of the true state of affairs. A statement which is true when made but which becomes untrue may also be a misrepresentation. In *Corner* v *Mundy* [1987] CLY 479 there was a correct statement in replies to inquiries that the central heating was in good working order. Before exchange the system froze and was damaged and that fact was not reported to the buyer. The seller was liable for damages in misrepresentation.

Remedies

A misrepresentation may be fraudulent, negligent or innocent, and the remedies available depend on the nature of the misrepresentation

Fraudulent
A misrepresentation is fraudulent if the person who makes it knows that it is false or is reckless as to whether it is true or false. If fraudulent misrepresentation is proved, then the innocent party can rescind the contract and claim damages in tort for deceit: *Derry* v *Peek* (1889) 14 AC 337. To allege and prove fraud is difficult and therefore it is more usual to claim for negligent misrepresentation.

Negligent

A misrepresentation will be made negligently if the seller cannot prove that he had reasonable grounds for believing the truth of what he said and did so believe up to the time the contract was made: s2(1) Misrepresentation Act 1967. The remedies are that the innocent party can claim damages and/or rescission, although the court may award damages in lieu of rescission.

Innocent

A misrepresentation is innocent if the seller can prove that he did have reasonable grounds for believing that what he said was true and did so believe. An aggrieved party can only claim rescission for innocent misrepresentation but the court can award damages in lieu.

Rescission

In the context of misrepresentation, rescission is an equitable remedy which is discretionary and is granted on the basis of equitable principles. The usual bars, such as delay, are applicable. Also, if third parties have acquired rights the right to rescind is lost as restitutio in integrum is no longer possible. Thus, if a purchaser has mortgaged the property the right to rescind will be lost as the mortgagee will have acquired rights in the property. The purpose of rescission is to put the parties in the position they would have been in if the contract had not been entered into. In relation to negligent or innocent misrepresentation the court may decide to award damages in lieu of rescission. In most cases it is likely that the court will do so as rescission would be a drastic remedy and the loss suffered by a purchaser will be able to be adequately compensated by a monetary payment. It would normally only be where a purchaser has been completely deprived of his bargain as a result of the misrepresentation that rescission would be allowed.

Standard Condition 7.1 also applies to misrepresentation. Where an incorrect statement is made in the negotiations leading to the contract, the injured party is entitled to damages if there is a material difference between the value of the property as described and as it is: SC 7.1.2. An error or omission entitles an injured party to rescind only if he would have to accept property differing substantially from that which he expected or if the false statement is made fraudulently or recklessly: SC 7.1.3. This provision restricts the remedies available for misrepresentation and as such has to satisfy the test of reasonableness contained in the Unfair Contract Terms Act 1977: s3 Misrepresentation Act 1967. It should be noted that there is no restriction on the remedies available if there is a fraudulent or negligent misrepresentation. Certain forms and documents also contain disclaimers or exclusion clauses. For example, some preliminary inquiry forms may contain exclusion clauses, although the forms used under the Conveyancing Protocol do not, but any such clause would also have to satisfy the test of reasonableness.

14

Leases

14.1 Introduction

Although in many cases a conveyancing transaction will be dealing with a freehold property and the sale of the fee simple, this will not always be the case as leases are also the subject of a conveyancing transaction. Reference should be made to standard land law textbooks for details of leasehold property, but here will be outlined the significant differences between freehold and leasehold conveyancing.

Although leases of dwelling-houses may be met, most leases nowadays relate either to commercial property – shops, offices, factories, farms, etc – or residential flats. From a landlord's point of view there are advantages in leases. For example, he may charge a premium (a capital sum on the grant of a lease) and/or rent to produce an income, and he can exercise control over property through leasehold covenants. In particular, positive covenants can be enforced against successors in title, whereas in freehold land only the burden of restrictive covenants can run with the land. This is one reason why freehold flats are uncommon. From the tenant's view, however, there are distinct disadvantages with leasehold property. He may be under greater control about what he can do with the property, there may be restrictions on sale, and the lease is a wasting asset as it is for a finite period.

There are two transactions in leasehold conveyancing which need to be identified:

1. the grant of a lease, where the leasehold estate is created;

2. the assignment of a lease, involving the transfer of a lease which is already in existence, ie the transfer of an existing legal estate.

14.2 The grant of a lease

The grant of a lease is the creation of a lease out of either a freehold or existing leasehold interest. In the latter case it will be a sub-lease and the tenant under the head lease will become the landlord under the sub-lease.

Contract

If there is a contract this will be drawn up by the landlord who will also prepare the draft lease. Although there will often be a contract stage, it is not unusual in leasehold conveyancing for there to be no contract but for the parties to proceed directly to completion. The lease will contain terms such as length, rent, covenants for insurance, repairs and user. The terms of the lease are a matter of negotiation between the parties. If there is a contract the draft lease will be annexed to the contract, and the contract will be in the form that the parties will enter into the lease in accordance with the draft annexed to the contract.

The pre contract package will contain the following:

1. contract (if there is one);
2. draft lease;
3. planning permissions, etc;
4. property information form, etc;
5. any other relevant documentation.

Covenants for title – full or limited title guarantee – will be given, except where the lease is short.

Title

The open contract rule is that on the grant of a lease a tenant is not entitled to call for evidence of the landlord's title: s44(2) LPA. This is unsatisfactory, particularly if the lease if for a long period, a substantial premium is being demanded or the lease is to be used as security. If the lease is to be registered, in the absence of proof of the landlord's title only a good leasehold title will be granted. On the grant of lease, therefore, if the tenant wishes for evidence of the landlord's title there must be a contractual provision to that effect. Standard Condition 8.2.4 alters the open contract position. Where there is the grant of a new lease which will exceed 21 years the landlord has to provide such evidence as will enable the tenant to be registered with absolute title. Leases granted for over 21 years trigger first registration of title. In the absence of evidence of the landlord's title only good leasehold title will be granted. If the lease is for less than 21 years this provision will not apply and if in that case the tenant wishes for proof of the landlord's title then a special condition to that effect must be included in the contract. Of course, if the lease is granted out of a registered title evidence of the landlord's title will be available in the form of office copy entries whether or not such a condition is included.

Preliminary searches and inquiries

The tenant should carry out the same inquiries and searches as are done in freehold conveyancing. The exception is that in short leases, particularly of residential properties, full searches and investigations are not normally done.

Completion

The landlord will normally engross the lease, and there will usually be two copies. In readiness for completion the landlord will sign one copy – the lease – and the tenant the other copy – the counterpart. The tenant will carry out such pre-completion searches as are appropriate. On completion the tenant will hand over the signed counterpart to be kept by the landlord and the landlord will hand over the signed lease to be kept by the tenant. The tenant pays any money due and receives any other documents, eg examined copies of the landlord's title in unregistered land.

After completion

The tenant has to pay stamp duty unless the lease is exempt. The lease will have to be produced to the Inland Revenue and any duty paid. The lease is stamped with ad valorem stamp duty in accordance with a table based on length, premium and rent. The counterpart which is retained by the landlord also has to be produced to the authorities and stamped with the appropriate duty – 50p.

A lease granted for more than 21 years must be registered at HM Land Registry whether or not the title out of which it is granted is registered. If the landlord's title is registered the land or charge certificate will have been placed on deposit at the Land Registry with a deposit number and the grant of the new lease will be noted against the landlord's title. (The grant of a lease out of a registered title is a dealing and so the land or charge certificate needs to be produced to the Land Registry for the dealing to be registered.) The lease is not kept at the Registry, or included in the certificate, but is returned to the tenant.

14.3 Assignment of a lease

In large measure, the assignment of a lease is the same as the sale of a freehold, in that it is the transfer of an existing legal estate, save that the estate which is transferred is a term of years and not a fee simple. The lease is in existence and the terms are not open for negotiation; what will be transferred to the purchaser is the residue of the existing lease, with all the terms as they are.

Contract

This will be in many respects the same as the contract for the sale of a freehold estate. It will be prepared by the seller's solicitor, and it will deal with similar issues to those in relation to freehold land. The assignor will on an assignment give the covenants for title implied by limited or full title guarantee in relation to a sale of freehold land. In addition, under s4 of the Law of Property (Miscellaneous Provisions) Act 1994, where there is an assignment of a lease, and whether full or limited title guarantee is given, there are implied covenants:

1. that at the time of the disposition the lease is subsisting;
2. that there is no breach of the tenant's covenants and that he has done nothing that would render the lease liable to forfeiture.

Standard Condition 3.2.2, however, modifies this and states that the property is sold subject to any subsisting breach of condition or tenant's obligation relating to the physical condition of the property which render the lease liable to forfeiture.

Title

The evidence of title which the seller has to provide will, if the title is unregistered, be the lease, however old, as this is the document which creates the estate being transferred, and the devolution of that estate for at least 15 years prior to the sale will have to be proved in the same way as the devolution of a freehold estate is proved. Thus, any assignments, mortgages, devolution on death, etc for a period of at least 15 years will have to be abstracted. If the lease is registered, the office copy entries of the register and the lease will constitute the title.

The purchaser cannot call for evidence of the landlord's title. If the lease is to be the subject of first registration following the assignment, in order to obtain absolute title the landlord's title will have to be proved. If the seller himself has not got the evidence, then he will not be able to provide the evidence which will enable this to be done. If the landlord's freehold title is registered then this can, however, be achieved.

Purchaser's inquiries and searches

These will be the same as in relation to freehold. Under the Conveyancing Protocol the seller prepares a pre-contract package in the same way as for freehold. This will contain the draft contract, the lease, evidence of title, planning permissions etc, property information forms, consents to assign. In addition, the purchaser will wish to see receipts for the last instalments of rent, service charges, etc, will wish to ensure that any insurance is in force and that there are no outstanding breaches of covenant on the part of the seller.

Completion

After exchange of contracts the matter proceeds to completion. The assignment is the document which transfers the estate and this will normally be prepared by the purchaser in the same way that the purchaser prepares a freehold conveyance. The appropriate pre-completion searches will have to be made. One matter which has to be dealt with in relation to leases is apportionments. Payments such as rent, service charges and insurance have to be made by the tenant. These may be paid either in advance or in arrears. If payments are made in advance then the seller will already have paid them and on completion the purchaser will have to pay a sum representing that part of the payments in advance which will be attributable to the purchaser's period of ownership. Similarly, if payments are made in arrears, then an allowance has to be made against the purchase price in relation to that sum which the purchaser will in due course pay which is attributable to the period of the seller's ownership.

After completion

After completion the purchaser will have to deal with the stamp duty formalities in the same way as the sale of a freehold. Stamp duty is payable ad valorem on the consideration for the assignment. If the lease is registered, then the transfer will have to be registered in the usual way at the Land Registry, again bearing in mind the priority period of any search. If the assignment is of an unregistered lease with over 21 years left to run, then that triggers first registration of title.

If the lease requires notice of assignment to be given to the landlord, then the purchaser will also have to deal with that.

14.4 Statutory intervention

In dealing with leasehold conveyancing, the statutory provisions relating to landlord and tenant must be borne in mind. Reference should be made to standard textbooks for the details on this very complicated subject, but some of the more important issues are outlined below:

Residential property

Tenants of residential property have protection under a variety of statutes. A tenancy at a market rent may be an assured tenancy under the Housing Acts. These impose some controls over the rent which can be charged and give the tenant security of tenure in accordance with the Acts. In granting a tenancy care needs to be taken to ensure that the right formalities are observed and the correct form of residential tenancy is created.

Of particular significance in a conveyancing context is the Leasehold Reform Act 1967. Under this, the lessee of a dwelling-house let under a long lease with at least 50 years left to run can compel the landlord either to sell the freehold (at market value) or grant a new lease. This Act only applies to houses and not to flats. There are a variety of other provisions in force relating to flats. In particular, under the Leasehold Reform, Housing and Urban Development Act 1993 tenants in a block of flats can together decide to buy the freehold, and they can compel the landlord to sell the freehold at market value to a management company in which they will hold shares, and the tenants thereby become in effect their own landlords.

Business property

Under the Landlord and Tenant Act 1954 tenants of business properties are given protection. The Act lays down procedures which a landlord has to follow if he wishes to regain possession at the end of a lease, by specifying the form of notices, the grounds on which possession can be obtained and time limits, and it gives the tenant the right to apply to the court for an order granting a new tenancy if the landlord will not give one. It also gives a tenant a right to compensation in some circumstances if the landlord resumes possession. It is possible to contract out of the security of tenure provisions but only with the permission of the court and therefore if it is desired to exclude the 1954 Act provisions from a business tenancy, a court order to that effect has to be obtained before the lease is concluded.

Agricultural property

Leases of farms entered into before 1995 are subject to the Agricultural Holdings Act 1986. This gave tenants security of tenure by limiting the grounds on which a landlord could regain possession. It set out formal procedures with time limits which had to be followed, gave an evicted tenant a right to compensation in some circumstances and imposed a statutory framework over the relationship of landlord and tenant. It was felt that this Act was unduly restrictive and was a disincentive to landlords and so the law was reformed by the Rent (Agriculture) Act 1995. Any tenancy granted after 1995 will not come under the Agricultural Holdings Act with the statutory controls. It will instead be a farm business tenancy, with the only restriction on the landlords' ability to regain possession being the requirement of two years' notice. Again, in some circumstances, when a landlord regains possession a tenant may be entitled to compensation.

14.5 Leasehold covenants

On the assignment of a lease one issue which needs to be addressed is that of liability for covenants. There was a significant change made to the law in 1995 by the Landlord and Tenant (Covenants) Act. This only applies to leases granted after 1 January 1996, and therefore in order to establish which rules apply the date of the lease first has to be identified.

Pre-1996 leases

The original landlord and tenant remain liable under the terms of the lease for the whole of the term, even though they may have parted with all interest in the property which is the subject of the lease, as the lease is, inter alia, a contract between them. When a lease is assigned the assignee becomes liable under the terms of the lease to the landlord by virtue of the doctrine of privity of estate in relation to those covenants which touch and concern the land, ie have reference to the subject matter of the lease or alternatively relate to the relationship of landlord and tenant, which in most leases will be all the covenants in the lease: s141(1) LPA. Similarly, a landlord's obligations will run with the reversion: s142 LPA. An assignee will not be liable under covenants once he himself has assigned the lease unless he himself is under a continuing liability, eg if he has entered into a direct covenant with the landlord to observe and perform the terms of the lease. Where an assignor remains under liability after he has parted with the property, then the issue of an indemnity covenant needs to be considered.

Example

L grants a lease for 30 years in 1980 to T. L and T are both liable in relation to the covenants for the whole of the term. In 1993 T assigns to A. T remains liable under the covenants, but A also becomes liable. In this situation the primary liability is between L and A but T remains potentially liable. If A in due course assigns the lease to H, H becomes liable but A is under no liability in relation to breaches occurring after he parted with the property.

In such a situation, T can protect himself by taking an indemnity covenant in the assignment, ie when T assigns to A, A covenants with T to observe and perform the lease and to indemnify T against any claims in respect of the lease. Under s77(1)(c) LPA such a covenant is implied in an assignment for valuable consideration. In registered land such a covenant is implied by s24(1)(b) LRA in relation to all assignments whether or not for value.

Leases after 1996

It was increasingly felt that the above situation was not satisfactory as liability could attach to T years after he had disposed of the property and after a succession of assignments in relation to which he had no control. The Law Commission reported on this matter in 1988 (*Landlord and Tenant Law: Privity of Contract and Estate*, Law Com No 174) and in 1995 the Landlord and Tenant (Covenants) Act radically altered the law.

The essential features of the Act are as follows:

1. Section 3: Where a tenant assigns a lease the assignee becomes bound by the covenants in the lease except those which are purely personal to the assignor. There is a similar provision making the assignor of a reversion liable where the landlord assigns the reversion, and under s4 the landlord's right of re-entry passes with the reversion.

2. Section 5: Where a tenant assigns the lease he is released from all future liability under the covenants in the lease. This applies whether he is the original lessee or an assignee. The effect of this is that a tenant is only liable under a lease when he is the actual lessee. Once he has assigned the lease, then he is under no further liability. This release operates as a matter of law and does not require any action by the parties.

3. Section 6: Where a landlord assigns the reversion he is not automatically released from his covenants, but he may apply to the tenant to be released from his covenants (the new landlord of course becoming liable under s3). If the tenant refuses to release the assignor he may apply to the court for an order for release.

4. Section 14: The implied indemnities under s77 LPA and s24 LRA are abolished

5. Section 25: This section makes any attempt to exclude the Act void.

Under the Act, the only way in which a tenant can remain liable under a lease after he has assigned it is if he enters into an authorised guarantee agreement. Under s16, if the lease requires the landlord's consent to an assignment, the landlord can impose a requirement that the tenant enters into an authorised guarantee agreement. This is an agreement whereby the assignor guarantees the performance of the lease by his assignee only and no further.

Example
In 1998 L grants a lease to T. In 2000 T assigns to A. T is released from all continuing liability under the lease, and A becomes liable. In 2002 A assigns to H. A is released from all future liability under the lease. The only way in which T can remain liable under the lease is if L is entitled to call for an authorised guarantee agreement, and he will only be able to do so if the assignment requires his consent. If his consent is required L can state that as a condition of authorising the assignment from T to A, T shall enter into a guarantee in relation to A's performance of the lease. Such an agreement cannot impose liability in relation to H's performance, as it can only relate to the assignor's own assignee. As a condition of giving consent to the assignment from A to H, L could require A to enter into a guarantee in relation to H's observance of the lease.

14.6 Consent to assignment

The lease may impose restrictions on the tenant's ability to transfer a lease, either by means of an absolute prohibition or by the imposition of a requirement that the landlord has to consent to an assignment. If there is no such provision in the lease the lease is freely assignable. If the landlord wishes to retain control over who will be his tenant he must make provision in the lease. If there is an absolute prohibition on assignment, an assignment in contravention of this provision is effective but renders the lease liable to forfeiture. Where there is such a prohibition the tenant can ask the landlord for his consent to an assignment, and it is entirely within the landlord's discretion whether or not he wishes to grant it. Much more common is a covenant requiring the tenant to obtain the landlord's consent to an assignment. Under s19 Landlord and Tenant Act 1927 in such a case there is implied a provision that the consent will not be withheld unreasonably. Refusal on the grounds of sex or race is automatically unreasonable. The landlord may require references, including banker's and trade references, may require a surety if, for example, the proposed assignee is a limited company, or may require an authorised guarantee agreement. The landlord may also require the assignee to enter into a direct covenant to observe and perform the terms of the lease. The landlord is under a duty to give a decision within a reasonable time, and must serve a notice specifying the conditions required or giving reasons for refusal to consent. Breach of this duty by a landlord is actionable.

Standard Condition 8.3 deals with the issue of landlord's consent.

If the landlord's consent is necessary the seller has to apply for it at his expense and use all reasonable efforts to obtain it, and the buyer has to provide all references and information reasonably required. If within three working days of completion consent has not been given, or has been given subject to unreasonable conditions, either party, unless he has failed to carry out the obligations set out above, may rescind the contract. If that is done, neither party is to be treated as in breach and any deposit paid by the purchaser is to be returned and the buyer is to return any documents and cancel any registration.

14.7 Sub-leases

A lease is a lease granted out of a freehold, whereas a sub-lease is a lease granted out of a leasehold.

The following are the more significant differences applicable to sub-leases:

1. On the grant of a sub-lease, the sub-tenant can call for the head lease out of which the sub-lease is to be granted, and all assignments of the lease for at least 15 years. A sub-tenant is not entitled to call for the deduction of the freehold title. Standard Condition 8.2.4 applies to sub-leases and so if a sub-lease is

granted for a term of over 21 years evidence to enable an absolute title will have to be provided unless this provision is excluded by a special condition. If the head-lease is itself registered then production of the freehold title will not be necessary

2. Assignment of a sub-lease. If unregistered, the lease and at least 15 years devolution must be produced but under the open contract rules the assignee cannot call for evidence of the freehold title. Again, if there is at least 21 years left to run, the assignment will trigger first registration

3. Under a sub-lease there is no direct relationship between the landlord under the head-lease and the sub-tenant. The landlord has the tenant under the head lease as his tenant, and that tenant in turn is the landlord under the sub-lease.

4. A lease may contain restrictions on the granting of sub-leases similar to those relating to assignments – prohibition or a requirement of consent. The above provisions relating to consents to assignments apply to consents to sub-letting.

5. Standard Condition 3.2.3 states that a sub-lease is granted subject to any subsisting breach of condition or tenant's obligation relating to the physical state of the property which renders the seller's lease liable to forfeiture.

15

Mortgages

15.1 Introduction

15.2 Bankruptcy searches

15.3 Creation of mortgages

15.4 Undue influence

15.1 Introduction

The definition of purchase in the LPA includes a mortgage, and there are particular problems which need to be addressed when a mortgage of property is being considered.

A mortgagee has security over property in respect of indebtedness, and in the event of default by the mortgagor, the mortgagee has various remedies, including the ability to take possession and sell. When a mortgage is being granted the mortgagee wishes to ensure that in the event of default by the mortgagor he will be able to sell the property and recover what is due. He is therefore concerned to ensure that the mortgagor has a good title which will be readily saleable and will carry out the same investigations – searches, inquiries, requisitions, etc – as are carried out by a buyer when purchasing property. In many cases a mortgage is created at the same time as a purchaser buys property, and the mortgage advance is used to pay the purchase price. In such a case the purchaser reviews the draft contract, carries out preliminary searches and inquiries, raises requisitions on title and does necessary pre-completion searches. A mortgagee needs to carry out similar investigations. A solicitor acting for a mortgagee has to ensure that the title is in order, prepare the mortgage documentation, ensure that the mortgage is completed and the mortgagee's legal position is protected and deal with any registration requirements. A mortgagee will normally have a valuation, to enable him to be satisfied that the property is adequate security for the money which is to be secured. This is less thorough than an purchaser's survey: see Chapter 5, section 5.3.

The importance of a valuation was emphasised in *Banque Bruxelles Lambert SA v Eagle Star Insurance Co Ltd* [1995] 2 WLR 607 where the court held that where valuers had negligently valued property in connection with a mortgage, and but for the negligent valuation the lender would not have entered into the transaction at all, the lender could recover from the valuers losses resulting from a subsequent fall in the property market.

Because a mortgagee and purchaser will carry out many similar investigations, to avoid unnecessary duplication it is normal, where there is a contemporaneous purchase and mortgage, at least in connection with ordinary residential conveyancing, for the buyer's solicitor also to act on behalf of the mortgagee. The normal rule is that a solicitor can only act for one party to a transaction. There is a relaxation in relation to conveyancing transactions in that a solicitor can act for a mortgagor and mortgagee, provided that there is no conflict of interest. (For a detailed discussion of this reference should be made to works on solicitors' professional conduct.) There have been difficulties in the past over precisely what responsibilities a solicitor in this situation should undertake. This has now been resolved, and following discussions between mortgage lenders and the Law Society, a Lenders' Handbook has been issued containing a list of those matters in respect of which a solicitor can act if there is joint representation. If the lender's instructions are outside these matters then the solicitor is not permitted to act for the lender and borrower.

It is often the case that a mortgage is granted not simultaneously with a purchase but at some future time, in respect of property already owned by the mortgagor. If that is the case then the same inquiries as in relation to a purchase should be made – searches, inquiries, title investigation, etc. A solicitor may act for lender and borrower – again there is no problem if there is no conflict of interest and the responsibilities are within the scope of the Lenders' Handbook.

15.2 Bankruptcy searches

A buyer of property carries out investigations in respect of the property, the seller and the seller's title. As well as the normal investigations relating to the property, a mortgagee has to carry out investigations in relation to the mortgagor since it is the mortgagor who will be creating the mortgage. In particular, this involves checking the bankruptcy status of the mortgagor by means of a bankruptcy search at the Land Charges Registry against the mortgagor. If the property is unregistered, and the mortgage is not contemporaneous with a purchase, a mortgagee must carry out a full LCA search against the mortgagor which will reveal any bankruptcy entries. A bankruptcy search, which is a search of the Land Charges Register in relation to bankruptcy matters only, must be done by the mortgagee in relation to unregistered land when the sale is contemporaneous with a purchase (a full land charges search will in that case be done against the seller) or in any case where the land is registered. The bankruptcy search will reveal whether a bankruptcy petition has been issued or whether a bankruptcy order has been made: see Chapter 11, section 11.2.

Under s284 Insolvency Act 1986 if a person is made bankrupt any disposition made by him after the presentation of the petition without the leave of the court is void. This section does not, however, enable proceedings to be taken against any person who has received property from the bankrupt before the bankruptcy in good faith and for value and without notice of the petition. Bankruptcy petitions are registered under the LCA in the register of pending actions and therefore if a petition is registered that will be notice and a person will not be able to obtain the above protection.

As an example, on 31 January a bankruptcy petition is presented against M. On 31 March M buys a property from S and grants a mortgage in favour of B, a bank which lends him the purchase money which is paid to S. On 1 May M is declared bankrupt. Under s284 Insolvency Act 1986 the effect of the bankruptcy order made on 1 May is to avoid any disposition of property effected by M since 31 January, which includes the mortgage in favour of B unless B is acting in good faith, for value and without notice. If the bankruptcy petition has been registered, B loses his security as he will have notice. The money lent has been paid to S and is not recoverable from him so B will rank as an unsecured creditor in M's bankruptcy. In order to avoid this, B does a bankruptcy search against M in the period leading up to completion on 31 March. That search will reveal the petition if it is registered and warn B that any mortgage granted by M will be void if M is subsequently declared bankrupt. (If the petition is withdrawn then s284 does not apply, as it only comes into force on the bankruptcy.)

15.3 Creation of mortgages

A legal mortgage can be created by the grant of a long lease or by a charge by deed by way of legal mortgage; the latter is now the usual method. Prior to 1989 an equitable charge could be created by deposit of title deeds with a memorandum of deposit; after 1989 that is no longer possible and for an equitable charge to be created in this way the requirements of s2 of the Law of Property (Miscellaneous Provisions) Act 1989 will have to be satisfied: see Chapter 3, section 3.2.

In unregistered land, a legal mortgage where the mortgagee has the deeds does not have to be registered. A legal mortgage not protected by deposit of title deeds has to be protected by registration as a Class C(i) land charge (puisne mortgage) and an equitable mortgage will normally require protection by registration as a Class C(iii) land charge (general equitable charge). It should be borne in mind that after the 1997 Land Registration Act the granting of a legal mortgage where the mortgagee would obtain the deeds now triggers first registration of title.

If the title to land is registered all charges have to be completed by registration.

15.4 Undue influence

A particular area of difficulty in recent years has been in relation to undue influence. especially following the case of *Barclays Bank plc* v *O'Brien* [1992] 4 All ER 983. Typically, a wife who is a co-owner or sole owner of a house charges the property in favour of a third party to secure the debts of her husband. The creation of the mortgage is a conveyancing transaction but the issues of misrepresentation, duress and undue influence have to be considered. In this situation, in what circumstances will the lender not be able to rely on the security because it was procured by the husband's undue influence or misrepresentation?

It has long been established that a transaction which is procured by duress or undue influence is voidable. Undue influence can be classified as follows:

* Class 1 – actual undue influence;
* Class 2 – presumed undue influence established by proving the existence of a relationship of trust and confidence subdivided as follows:
* Class 2A – those relationships which are as a matter of law relationships of trust and confidence;
* Class 2B – where it is established by evidence that the complainant reposed trust and confidence in the wrongdoer.

In this situation, therefore, as between the husband and wife, if there is a vitiating factor the transaction is voidable. In dealing with the lender's position, however, the issue is not simply whether there was undue influence, etc, but whether the lender had notice of it. A lender will normally be put on notice of the fact that a wife might be able to have a transaction set aside by a combination of two factors – that the transaction is not on the face of it to the wife's advantage and that there is a substantial risk that the husband had obtained the wife's consent by undue influence. If a lender is aware of these facts then it can normally protect itself by ensuring that the wife has independent legal advice. If legal advice is given, whether the bank can enforce its rights against the wife depends, first, on whether the advice given was such as to rebut any suggestion of undue influence and, second, whether in the light of the facts known to the bank any risk of the wife being able to allege undue influence had been dispelled. There is no requirement that the transaction be to the wife's disadvantage, although if it is that will be strong evidence of undue influence. In *Royal Bank of Scotland* v *Ettridge (No 2)* [1998] 4 All ER 705 the Court of Appeal laid down guidelines. Where a wife deals with a lender through a solicitor the lender will not normally be put on inquiry and can assume that the wife is being adequately advised. The bank can normally rely on the fact that the solicitor undertook to advise the wife and is not concerned to question whether the advice given was adequate. In *Bank of Scotland* v *Bennett* [1999] Lloyd's Rep Bank 145, for example, a wife charged the family home to secure the overdraft of a company run by her husband. The bank asked the husband's solicitors to deal with matters. The judge held that on the facts there was undue influence but the issue was whether the bank had notice of it. He held that in the absence of particular facts, a transaction in which a wife guaranteed the debts of her husband's business which provided the family income could not be said to be improvident. The bank could assume that the solicitor would advise the wife on all relevant matters. In *Woolwich Building Society* v *Gomm* (1999) The Times 21 September a woman charged a property to secure her ex-husband's debts and acting under the undue influence of her ex-husband transferred her house into the joint names of herself and a third party; the ex-husband in fact forged the other party's signature. The solicitors acted for all parties – the wife, the third party and the lender. There was undoubtedly undue influence on the part of the ex-husband and the transactions were voidable, but the question was whether the lender had notice. The court held that the transaction had to be looked at from the lender's point of view (and the knowledge which the solicitor obtained in acting as the wife's solicitor was not imputed to the lender) and in this case there was no need for further inquiry as the transaction was not on the face of it improvident or to the wife's disadvantage.

The effect of this approach is that as long as lenders have ensured that a wife has legal advice they can assume that the matter has been dealt with correctly and the wife had been appropriately advised and they will be able to enforce the charge. As between the husband and wife the transaction may well be voidable but that does not affect the lender. In such a situation, if the wife's position has not been adequately protected she may in due course be able to claim against her solicitor for inadequate advice.

Appendices

Appendix 1

Edition date 25 October 1993   **TITLE NUMBER WE 14095**

Entry No	A. PROPERTY REGISTER *containing the description of the registered land and the estate comprised in the Title*
	COUNTY KENT DISTRICT BARCHESTER
1.	(23 August 1988) The Freehold land shown edged with red on the plan of the above Title filed at the Registry and being 24 Empire Avenue, Barchester, Wessex.
2.	(25 October 1993) The land has the benefit of a right of way on foot only over the pathway shown coloured brown on the filed plan.

Entry No	B. PROPRIETORSHIP REGISTER *stating nature of the Title, name, address and description of the proprietor of the land and any entries affecting the right of disposing thereof* **TITLE ABSOLUTE**
1.	(25 October 1993) Proprietors: Michael Keith Hill and Winifred Doris Hill both of 24 Empire Avenue, Barchester, Wessex.
2.	(25 October 1993) RESTRICTION: No disposition by a sole proprietor of the land (not being a trust corporation) under which capital money arises is to be registered except under an order of the Registrar or the Court.

Entry No	C. CHARGES REGISTER *containing charges, incumbrances etc, adversely affecting the land and registered dealings therewith*
1.	(23 August 1988) A Conveyance of the land in this title dated 24 July 1956 between Brian Brown and Regal Properties Ltd contains restrictive covenants. (Copy in Certificate.)
2.	(25 October 1993) CHARGE dated 15 August 1993 to secure the monies including further advances therein mentioned.
3.	PROPRIETOR: Friendly Building Society of Friendly House, High Street, Northtown, Wyeshire.

Appendix 2

Appendix 2 comprises a typical contract, in blank form, together with a completed example.

Reproduced by kind permission of the Law Society of England and Wales and the Solicitors' Law Stationery Society Limited for educational purposes only.

AGREEMENT

(Incorporating the Standard Conditions of Sale (Third Edition))

Agreement date   :

Seller   :

Buyer   :

Property   :
(freehold/leasehold)

Root of title/Title Number   :

Incumbrances on the Property :

Title Guarantee   :
(full/limited)

Completion date   :

Contract rate   :

Purchase price   :

Deposit   :

Amount payable for chattels :

Balance   :

The Seller will sell and the Buyer will buy the Property for the Purchase price.
The Agreement continues on the back page.

WARNING	Signed
This is a formal document, designed to create legal rights and legal obligations. Take advice before using it.	
	Seller/Buyer

SPECIAL CONDITIONS

1. (a) This agreement incorporates the Standard Conditions of Sale (Third Edition)
   Where there is a conflict between those Conditions and this Agreement, this Agreement prevails.

   (b) Terms used or defined in this Agreement have the same meaning when used in the Standard Conditions of Sale.

2. The Property is sold subject to the Incumbrances on the Property and the Buyer will raise no requisitions on them.

3. Subject to the terms of this Agreement and to the Standard Conditions of Sale, the seller is to transfer the property with the title guarantee specified on the front page.

4. The chattels on the Property and set out on any attached list are included in the sale.

5. [The Property is sold with vacant possession on completion.]

(or)　　　[The Property is sold subject to the following leases or tenancies:]

Seller's Solicitors　　　　　:

Buyer's Solicitors　　　　　:

AGREEMENT

(Incorporating the Standard Conditions of Sale (Third Edition))

Agreement date	:	9th July 2000
Seller	:	George Brian Mitchell of 49, Lowell Street, Singleton Mercia. SG2 4TH
Buyer	:	Lionel Henry Green and Marion Kate Green both of Flat 1, Anchor House, Ship Lane, Seaton, Southshire. SE7 4PP
Property (freehold/~~leasehold~~)	:	Freehold property known as 49 Lowell Street, Singleton, Mercia. SG2 4TH
~~Root of title~~/Title Number	:	Registered with absolute title at the Southsea District Land Registry under title number ME129856
Incumbrances on the Property	:	The covenants referred to in entry number 1 of the Charges Register of the above title.
Title Guarantee (full/limited)	:	The seller will sell with full title guarantee
Completion date	:	20th July 2000
Contract rate	:	The Law Society's Rate
Purchase price	:	£75 000
Deposit	:	£7500
Amount payable for chattels	:	£900
Balance	:	£68 400

The Seller will sell and the Buyer will buy the Property for the Purchase price.
The Agreement continues on the back page.

WARNING	Signed
This is a formal document, designed to create legal rights and legal obligations. Take advice before using it.	 Seller/Buyer

SPECIAL CONDITIONS

1. (a) This agreement incorporates the Standard Conditions of Sale (Third Edition))
   Where there is a conflict between those Conditions and this Agreement, this Agreement prevails.

   (b) Terms used or defined in this Agreement have the same meaning when used in the Standard Conditions of Sale.

2. The Property is sold subject to the Incumbrances on the Property and the Buyer will raise no requisitions on them.

3. Subject to the terms of this Agreement and to the Standard Conditions of Sale, the seller is to transfer the property with the title guarantee specified on the front page.

4. The chattels on the Property and set out on any attached list are included in the sale.

5. [The Property is sold with vacant possession on completion.]

(or)   [The Property is sold subject to the following leases or tenancies.]

Seller's Solicitors   : Smith and Co
                             56 High Street,
                             Southtown,
                             Wessex

                             Ref FGR/23

Buyer's Solicitors   : Lewis and Clark
                            4 Raven Court
                            Westville
                            Wessex

                            Ref: 1987/34

Laserform International 1/99

Appendix 3

EPITOME OF TITLE

Relating to freehold property known as 37 Morgan Crescent, Coketown, Gradshire.

No of Document	Document Date	Nature of Document or event	Parties	Abstract or Photocopy	Whether original will be handed over on completion
1	18 August 1960	Conveyance	(1) Michael George (2) Gordon Grant	A	No
2	18 August 1960	Mortgage (Receipt indorsed 26 June 1978)	(1) Gordon Grant (2) Gravity Building Society	A	No
3	27 June 1978	Deed of Gift	(1) Gordon Grant (2) Emily Grant	P	No
	13 November 1986	Death of Emily Grant			
4	12 January 1987	Examined copy Grant of Probate (Memorandum of assent indorsed)	Roger Grant and Guy Stephens	P	No
5	1 October 1987	Assent	(1) Roger Grant Guy Stephens (2) Guy Stephens	P	Yes
6	10 April 1988	Conveyance	(1) Guy Stephens (2) Clive Charles	P	Yes
7	10 April 1988	Legal Charge	(1) Clive Charles (2) Big Bank plc	P	Yes

Notes
1. The Conveyance dated 18 August 1960 is the root of title.
2. The Land Charges Registry search certificates have not been included.
3. The deed of gift is over five years old therefore issues of insolvency need not be considered.
4. Receipt indorsed on mortgage of 18 August 1960.
5. Memorandum of assent indorsed on probate.
6. The mortgage of 10 April 1988 is still subsisting and will have to be discharged on completion.

Appendix 4

THIS CONVEYANCE is made the 26th day of May 1995 BETWEEN SAMUEL GRAHAM PORTER and HELEN SUSAN PORTER both of 77 Leigh Avenue, Steeple Camden, Wessex (hereinafter called 'the Vendors') of the one part and MICHAEL GEORGE GREEN and GWYNETH LOUISE GREEN both of Flat 3, Morris House, Poole Avenue, Grantchester, Wessex (hereinafter called 'the Purchasers') of the other part

WHEREAS:

(1) The Vendors are seised of the property hereinafter described and hereby conveyed for an estate in fee simple in possession subject as hereinafter mentioned but otherwise free from incumbrances

(2) The Vendors have agreed with the Purchasers for the sale to them of the said property at a price of £55,000 (FIFTY-FIVE THOUSAND POUNDS)

NOW THIS DEED WITNESSETH AS FOLLOWS

1. In consideration of the said sum of £55,000 (FIFTY-FIVE THOUSAND POUNDS) now paid by the Purchasers to the Vendors (the receipt whereof the Vendors hereby acknowledge) the Vendors with full title guarantee HEREBY CONVEY unto the Purchasers ALL THAT freehold piece or parcel of land being part of the garden to the rear of 77 Leigh Avenue, Steeple Camden, Wessex known as Plot 1 77 Leigh Avenue Steeple Camden Wessex more particularly delineated on the plan annexed hereto and thereon edged in red TOGETHER WITH those rights set out in the Second Schedule hereto and EXCEPT AND RESERVED to the Vendors and their successors in title the owners and occupiers for the time being of the land shown edged blue on the plan annexed hereto (hereinafter called 'the Retained Land') the rights set out in the Third Schedule hereto TO HOLD the same unto the Purchasers in fee simple SUBJECT to the Covenants contained in the Conveyance described in the First Schedule hereto insofar as the same affect the property hereby conveyed and are still subsisting and capable of taking effect.

2. THE PURCHASERS HEREBY JOINTLY AND SEVERALLY COVENANT by way of indemnity with the Vendors that they and the persons deriving title under them will observe and perform the covenants contained in the said conveyance described in the First Schedule hereto so far as the same affect the property hereby conveyed and are still subsisting and capable of taking effect and will keep the Vendors and their estates and effects indemnified against all actions claims demands and liabilities arising as result of any future breach or non-observance or non-performance thereof.

3. IT IS HEREBY AGREED AND DECLARED that the Purchasers shall not by implication or otherwise become entitled to any right of light or air which would restrict or interfere with the use of the Retained Land for building or any other purpose.

4. FOR the benefit and protection of the Retained Land or any part thereof and so

as to bind the property hereby conveyed the Purchasers HEREBY JOINTLY AND SEVERALLY COVENANT with the Vendors that they the Purchasers and the persons deriving title under them will at all times hereafter observe and perform the covenants set out in the Fourth Schedule hereto.

5. THE PURCHASERS HEREBY DECLARE that they hold the property hereby conveyed and the net proceeds of sale and the net income from it until sale on trust for themselves as beneficial joint tenants.

6. THE VENDORS HEREBY ACKNOWLEDGE the right of the Purchasers to the production of a Conveyance dated 10th October 1967 and made between Lawrence Martin Gilbert of the one part and the Vendors of the other part and UNDERTAKE for the safe custody of the same.

7. IT IS HEREBY CERTIFIED that the transaction hereby effected does not form part of a larger transaction or series of transactions in respect of which the amount or value or the aggregate amount or value of the consideration exceeds £60,000.

IN WITNESS whereof the parties hereto have executed this deed the day and year first above written

FIRST SCHEDULE

Date	Document	Parties
1st May 1923	Conveyance	JB Smith (1)
		FC Wilson (2)

SECOND SCHEDULE

1. The free and uninterrupted right of way at all times and for all purposes with or without vehicles over the driveway shown coloured brown on the plan annexed hereto subject to the Purchasers paying a fair proportion according to usage of the cost of repairing and maintaining the said driveway.

2. The right to the free and uninterrupted passage of water through the pipe to be laid in the position shown with a dotted black line on the plan annexed hereto and the right upon giving reasonable notice except in case of emergency to enter onto the Retained Land to inspect maintain and repair the said pipe and upon making good any damage thereby caused.

THIRD SCHEDULE

1. The right to the free and uninterrupted passage of soil and gas through the pipes and sewers laid under the property hereby conveyed or to be laid within the period of eighty years subject to the Vendors paying a fair proportion of the cost of repairing and maintaining the same.

2. The right upon giving reasonable notice except in the case of emergencies to enter upon the property hereby conveyed to inspect maintain and repair the said pipes and sewers and upon making good any damage thereby caused.

FOURTH SCHEDULE

1. Any building erected on the land hereby conveyed shall be used only for the purpose of a private dwelling in the occupation of one family.

2. Nothing shall be done on the property hereby conveyed which shall be a nuisance or annoyance to the owners or occupiers of the Retained Land.

3. To erect and maintain a close boarded fence no higher than 2 metres along the boundary marked 'XY' on the plan annexed hereto.

Signed as a Deed by the said
SAMUEL GRAHAM PORTER
in the presence of:
Witness: Signature
           Name
           Address
           Occupation

Signed and witnessed by all parties

Signed as a deed by the said
HELEN SUSAN PORTER
in the presence of
Witness: Signature
           Name
           Address
           Occupation

Signed as a deed by the said
MICHAEL GEORGE GREEN
in the presence of
Witness: Signature
           Name
           Address
           Occupation

Signed as a deed by the said
GWYNETH LOUISE GREEN
in the presence of
Witness: Signature
           Name
           Address
           Occupation

Appendix 5

Appendix 5 comprises HM Land Registry Form TR1: Transfer of whole of registered title(s).

Crown copyright material is reproduced with kind permission of the Controller of Her Majesty's Stationery Office.

**Transfer of whole
of registered title(s)**

HM Land Registry

(if you need more room than is provided for in a panel, use continuation sheet CS and staple to this form)

1. Stamp Duty

Place "X" in the box that applies and complete the box in the appropriate certificate.

☐ I/We hereby certify that this instrument falls within category ☐ in the Schedule to the Stamp Duty (Exempt Instruments) Regulations 1987

☐ It is certified that the transaction effected does not form part of a larger transaction or of a series of transactions in respect of which the amount or value or the aggregate amount or value of the consideration exceeds the sum of

☐ £

2. Title Number(s) of the Property *(leave blank if not yet registered)*

3. Property

If this transfer is made under section 37 of the Land Registration Act 1925 following a not-yet-registered dealing with part only of the land in a title, or is made under rule 72 of the Land Registration Rules 1925, include a reference to the last preceding document of title containing a description of the property.

4. Date

5. Transferor *(give full names and Company's registered number if any)*

6. Transferee **for entry on the register** *(Give full names and Company's Registered Number if any; for Scottish Co. Reg. Nos., use an SC prefix. For foreign companies give territory in which incorporated.)*

Unless otherwise arranged with Land Registry headquarters, a certified copy of the transferee's constitution (in English or Welsh) will be required if it is a body corporate but is not a company registered in England and Wales or Scotland under the Companies Acts.

7. Transferee's intended **address(es) for service in the U.K.** *(including postcode)* **for entry on the register**

8. The Transferor transfers the property to the Transferee.

9. Consideration *(Place "X" in the box that applies. State clearly the currency unit if other than sterling. If none of the boxes applies, insert an appropriate memorandum in the additional provisions panel.)*

☐ The Transferor has received from the Transferee for the property the sum of *(in words and figures)*

☐ *(insert other receipt as appropriate)*

☐ The Transfer is not for money or anything which has a monetary value

10. The Transferor transfers with *(place "X" in the box which applies and add any modifications)*

☐ full title guarantee ☐ limited title guarantee

---

11. Declaration of trust *Where there is more than one transferee, place "X" in the appropriate box.*

☐ The transferees are to hold the property on trust for themselves as joint tenants.

☐ The transferees are to hold the property on trust for themselves as tenants in common in equal shares.

☐ The transferees are to hold the property *(complete as necessary)*

---

12. Additional Provision(s) *Insert here any required or permitted statement, certificate or application and any agreed covenants, declarations, etc.*

---

13. *The Transferors and all other necessary parties should execute this transfer as a deed using the space below. Forms of execution are given in Schedule 3 to the Land Registration Rules 1925. If the transfer contains transferees' covenants or declarations or contains an application by them (e.g. for a restriction), it must also be executed by the Transferees.*

Appendix 6

Standard Conditions of Sale (3rd edition 1995). Reproduced by kind permission of the Law Society of England and Wales and the Solicitors' Law Stationery Society Limited for educational purposes only.

(NATIONAL CONDITIONS OF SALE 23RD EDITION,
LAW SOCIETY'S CONDITIONS OF SALE 1995)

1. GENERAL

1.1 Definitions

1.1.1 In these conditions:
  (a) 'accrued interest' means:
     (i) if money has been placed on deposit or in a building society share account, the interest actually earned
     (ii) otherwise, the interest which might reasonably have been earned by depositing the money at interest on seven days' notice of withdrawal with a clearing bank

     less, in either case, any proper charges for handling the money
  (b) 'agreement' means the contractual document which incorporates these conditions, with or without amendment
  (c) 'banker's draft' means a draft drawn by and on a clearing bank
  (d) 'clearing bank' means a bank which is a member of CHAPS Limited
  (e) 'completion date', unless defined in the agreement, has the meaning given in condition 6.1.1
  (f) 'contract' means the bargain between the seller and the buyer of which these conditions, with or without amendment, form part
  (g) 'contract rate', unless defined in the agreement, is the Law Society's interest rate from time to time in force
  (h) 'lease' includes sub-lease, tenancy and agreement for a lease or sub-lease
  (i) 'notice to complete' means a notice requiring completion of the contract in accordance with condition 6
  (j) 'public requirement' means any notice, order or proposal given or made (whether before or after the date of the contract) by a body acting on statutory authority

131

    (k) 'requisition' includes objection

    (l) 'solicitor' includes barrister, duly certified notary public, recognised licensed conveyancer and recognised body under sections 9 or 32 of the Administration of Justice Act 1985

    (m) 'transfer' includes conveyance and assignment

    (n) 'working day' means any day from Monday to Friday (inclusive) which is not Christmas Day, Good Friday or a statutory Bank Holiday.

1.1.2 When used in these conditions the terms 'absolute title' and 'office copies' have the special meanings given to them by the Land Registration Act 1925.

1.2 *Joint parties*

If there is more than one seller or more than one buyer, the obligations which they undertake can be enforced against them all jointly or against each individually.

1.3 *Notices and documents*

1.3.1 A notice required or authorised by the contract must be in writing.

1.3.2 Giving a notice or delivering a document to a party's solicitor has the same effect as giving or delivering it to that party.

1.3.3 Transmission by fax is a valid means of giving a notice or delivering a document where delivery of the original document is not essential.

1.3.4 Subject to conditions 1.3.5 to 1.3.7, a notice is given and a document delivered when it is received.

1.3.5 If a notice or document is received after 4.00pm on a working day, or on a day which is not a working day, it is to be treated as having been received on the next working day.

1.3.6 Unless the actual time of receipt is proved, a notice or document sent by the following means is to be treated as having been received before 4.00pm on the day shown below:

    (a) by first-class post: two working days after posting

    (b) by second-class post: three working days after posting

    (c) through a document exchange: on the first working day after the day on which it would normally be available for collection by the addressee.

1.3.7 Where a notice or document is sent through a document exchange, then for the purposes of condition 1.3.6 the actual time of receipt is:

    (a) the time when the addressee collects it from the document exchange or, if earlier

(b) 8.00am on the first working day on which it is available for collection at that time.

1.4 *VAT*

1.4.1 An obligation to pay money includes an obligation to pay any value added tax chargeable in respect of that payment.
1.4.2 All sums made payable by the contract are exclusive of value added tax.

2. FORMATION

2.1 *Date*

2.1.1 If the parties intend to make a contract by exchanging duplicate copies by post or through a document exchange, the contract is made when the last copy is posted or deposited at the document exchange.
2.1.2 If the parties' solicitors agree to treat exchange as taking place before duplicate copies are actually exchanged, the contract is made as so agreed.

2.2 *Deposit*

2.2.1 The buyer is to pay or send a deposit of 10 per cent of the purchase price no later than the date of the contract. Except on a sale by auction, payment is to be made by banker's draft or by a cheque drawn on a solicitors' clearing bank account.
2.2.2 If before completion date the seller agrees to buy another property in England and Wales for his residence, he may use all or any part of the deposit as a deposit in that transaction to be held on terms to the same effect as this condition and condition 2.2.3.
2.2.3 Any deposit or part of a deposit not being used in accordance with condition 2.2.2 is to be held by the seller's solicitor as stakeholder on terms that on completion it is paid to the seller with accrued interest.
2.2.4 If a cheque tendered in payment of all or part of the deposit is dishonoured when first presented, the seller may, within seven working days of being notified that the cheque has been dishonoured, give notice to the buyer that the contract is discharged by the buyer's breach.

2.3 *Auctions*

2.3.1 On a sale by auction the following conditions apply to the property and, if it is sold in lots, to each lot.
2.3.2 The sale is subject to a reserve price.

2.3.3 The seller, or a person on his behalf, may bid up to the reserve price.

2.3.4 The auctioneer may refuse any bid.

2.3.5 If there is a dispute about a bid, the auctioneer may resolve the dispute or restart the auction at the last undisputed bid.

3. MATTERS AFFECTING THE PROPERTY

3.1 *Freedom from incumbrances*

3.1.1 The seller is selling the property free from incumbrances, other than those mentioned in condition 3.1.2.

3.1.2 The incumbrances subject to which the property is sold are:

(a) those mentioned in the agreement

(b) those discoverable by inspection of the property before the contract

(c) those the seller does not and could not know about

(d) entries made before the date of the contract in any public register except those maintained by HM Land Registry or its Land Charges Department or by Companies House

(e) public requirements.

3.1.3 After the contract is made, the seller is to give the buyer written details without delay of any new public requirement and of anything in writing which he learns about concerning any incumbrances subject to which the property is sold.

3.1.4 The buyer is to bear the cost of complying with any outstanding public requirement and is to indemnify the seller against any liability resulting from a public requirement.

3.2 *Physical state*

3.2.1 The buyer accepts the property in the physical state it is in at the date of the contract unless the seller is building or converting it.

3.2.2 A leasehold property is sold subject to any subsisting breach of a condition or tenant's obligation relating to the physical state of the property which renders the lease liable to forfeiture.

3.2.3 A sub-lease is granted subject to any subsisting breach of a condition or tenant's obligation relating to the physical state of the property which renders the seller's own lease liable to forfeiture.

3.3 *Leases affecting the property*

3.3.1 The following provisions apply if the agreement states that any part of the property is sold subject to a lease.

3.3.2 (a) The seller having provided the buyer with full details of each lease or copies of the documents embodying the lease terms, the buyer is treated as entering into the contract knowing and fully accepting those terms

(b) The seller is to inform the buyer without delay if the lease ends or if the seller learns of any application by the tenant in connection with the lease; the seller is then to act as the buyer reasonably directs, and the buyer is to indemnify him against all consequent loss and expense

(c) The seller is not to agree to any proposal to change the lease terms without the consent of the buyer and is to inform the buyer without delay of any change which may be proposed or agreed

(d) The buyer is to indemnify the seller against all claims arising from the lease after actual completion; this includes claims which are unenforceable against a buyer for want of registration

(e) The seller takes no responsibility for what rent is lawfully recoverable, nor for whether or how any legislation affects the lease

(f) If the let land is not wholly within the property, the seller may apportion the rent.

3.4   Retained land

3.4.1 The following provisions apply where after the transfer the seller will be retaining land near the property.

3.4.2 The buyer will have no right of light or air over the retained land, but otherwise the seller and the buyer will each have the rights over the land of the other which they would have had if they were two separate buyers to whom the seller had made simultaneous transfers of the property and the retained land.

3.4.3 Either party may require that the transfer contain appropriate express terms.

4. TITLE AND TRANSFER

4.1   Timetable

4.1.1 The following are the steps for deducing and investigating the title to the property to be taken within the following time limits:

Step	*Time limit*
1. The seller is to send the buyer evidence of title in accordance with condition 4.2	Immediately after making the contract
2. The buyer may raise written requisitions	Six working days after either the date of the contract or the date of

		delivery of the seller's evidence of title on which the requisitions are raised whichever is the later
3.	The seller is to reply in writing to any requisitions raised	Four working days after receiving requisitions
4.	The buyer may make written observations on the seller's replies	Three working days after receiving the replies

The time limit on the buyer's right to raise requisitions applies even where the seller supplies incomplete evidence of his title, but the buyer may, within six working days from delivery of any further evidence, raise further requisitions resulting from that evidence. On the expiry of the relevant time limit the buyer loses his right to raise requisitions or make observations.

4.1.2 The parties are to take the following steps to prepare and agree the transfer of the property within the following time limits:

	Step	*Time limit*
A.	The buyer is to send the seller a draft transfer	At least twelve working days before completion date
B.	The seller is to approve or revise that draft and either return it or retain it for use as the actual transfer	Four working days after delivery of the draft transfer
C.	If the draft is returned the buyer is to send an engrossment to the seller	At least five working days before completion date

4.1.3 Periods of time under conditions 4.1.1 and 4.1.2 may run concurrently.

4.1.4 If the period between the date of the contract and completion date is less than 15 working days, the time limits in conditions 4.1.1 and 4.1.2 are to be reduced by the same proportion as that period bears to the period of 15 working days. Fractions of a working day are to be rounded down except that the time limit to perform any step is not to be less than one working day.

4.2 *Proof of title*

4.2.1 The evidence of registered title is office copies of the items required to be furnished by section 110(1) of the Land Registration Act 1925 and the copies, abstracts and evidence referred to in section 110(2).

4.2.2 The evidence of unregistered title is an abstract of the title, or an epitome of title with photocopies of the relevant documents.

4.2.3 Where the title to the property is unregistered, the seller is to produce to the buyer (without cost to the buyer):

(a) the original of every relevant document, or

(b) an abstract, epitome or copy with an original marking by a solicitor of examination either against the original or against an examined abstract or against an examined copy.

4.3   Defining the property

4.3.1 The seller need not:
(a) prove the exact boundaries of the property

(b) prove who owns fences, ditches, hedges or walls

(c) separately identify parts of the property with different titles further than he may be able to do from information in his possession.

4.3.2 The buyer may, if it is reasonable, require the seller to make or obtain, pay for and hand over a statutory declaration about facts relevant to the matters mentioned in condition 4.3.1. The form of the declaration is to be agreed by the buyer, who must not unreasonably withhold his agreement.

4.4   Rents and rentcharges

The fact that a rent or rentcharge, whether payable or receivable by the owner of the property, has been or will on completion be, informally appointed is not to be regarded as a defect in title.

4.5   Transfer

4.5.1 The buyer does not prejudice his right to raise requisitions, or to require replies to any raised, by taking any steps in relation to the preparation or agreement of the transfer.

4.5.2 If the agreement makes no provision as to title guarantee, then subject to condition 4.5.3 the seller is to transfer the property with full title guarantee.

4.5.3 The transfer is to have effect as if the disposition is expressly made subject to all matters to which the property is sold subject under the terms of the contract.

4.5.4 If after completion the seller will remain bound by any obligation affecting the property, but the law does not imply any covenant by the buyer to indemnify the seller against liability for future breaches of it:

(a) the buyer is to covenant in the transfer to indemnify the seller against liability for any future breach of the obligation and to perform it from then on, and

(b) if required by the seller, the buyer is to execute and deliver to the seller on completion a duplicate transfer prepared by the buyer.

4.5.5 The seller is to arrange at his expense that, in relation to every document of title which the buyer does not receive on completion, the buyer is to have the benefit of:

(a) a written acknowledgement of his right to its production, and

(b) a written undertaking for its safe custody (except while it is held by a mortgagee or by someone in a fiduciary capacity).

5. PENDING COMPLETION

5.1 *Responsibility for property*

5.1.1 The seller will transfer the property in the same physical state as it was at the date of the contract (except for fair wear and tear), which means that the seller retains the risk until completion.

5.1.2 If at any time before completion the physical state of the property makes it unusable for its purpose at the date of the contract:

(a) the buyer may rescind the contract

(b) the seller may rescind the contract where the property has become unusable for the purpose as a result of damage against which the seller could not reasonably have insured, or which it is not legally possible for the seller to make good.

5.1.3 The seller is under no obligation to the buyer to insure the property.

5.1.4 Section 47 of the Law of Property Act 1925 does not apply.

5.2 *Occupation by buyer*

5.2.1 If the buyer is not already lawfully in the property, and the seller agrees to let him into occupation, the buyer occupies on the following terms.

5.2.2 The buyer is a licensee and not a tenant. The terms of the licence are that the buyer:

(a) cannot transfer it

(b) may permit members of his household to occupy the property

(c) is to pay or indemnify the seller against all outgoings and other expenses in respect of the property

(d) is to pay the seller a fee calculated at the contract rate on the purchase price (less any deposit paid) for the period of the licence

(e) is entitled to any rents and profits from any part of the property which he does not occupy

(f) is to keep the property in as good a state of repair as it was in when he went into occupation (except for fair wear and tear) and is not to alter it

(g) is to insure the property in a sum which is not less than the purchase price against all risks in respect of which comparable premises are normally insured

(h) is to quit the property when the licence ends.

5.2.3 On the creation of the buyer's licence, condition 5.1 ceases to apply, which means that the buyer then assumes the risk until completion.

5.2.4 The buyer is not in occupation for the purposes of this condition if he merely exercises rights of access given solely to do work agreed by the seller.

5.2.5 The buyer's licence ends on the earliest of: completion date, rescission of the contract or when five working days' notice given by one party to the other takes effect.

5.2.6 If the buyer is in occupation of the property after his licence has come to an end and the contract is subsequently completed he is to pay the seller compensation for his continued occupation calculated at the same rate as the fee mentioned in condition 5.2.2(d).

5.2.7 The buyer's right to raise requisitions is unaffected.

6. COMPLETION

6.1 *Date*

6.1.1 Completion date is twenty working days after the date of the contract but time is not of the essence of the contract unless a notice to complete has been served.

6.1.2 If the money due on completion is received after 2.00pm, completion is to be treated, for the purposes only of conditions 6.3 and 7.3, as taking place on the next working day.

6.1.3 Condition 6.1.2 does not apply where the sale is with vacant possession of the property or any part and the seller has not vacated the property or that part by 2.00pm on the date of actual completion.

6.2 *Place*

Completion is to take place in England and Wales, either at the seller's solicitor's office or at some other place which the seller reasonably specifies.

6.3 *Apportionment*

6.3.1 Income and outgoings of the property are to be apportioned between the parties so far as the change of ownership on completion will affect entitlement to receive or liability to pay them.

6.3.2 If the whole property is sold with vacant possession or the seller exercises his option in condition 7.3.4, apportionment is to be made with effect from the date of actual completion; otherwise, it is to be made from completion date.

6.3.3 In apportioning any sum, it is to be assumed that the seller owns the property until the end of the day from which apportionment is made and that the sum accrues from day to day at the rate at which it is payable on that day.

6.3.4 For the purpose of apportioning income and outgoings, it is to be assumed that they accrue at an equal daily rate throughout the year.

6.3.5 When a sum to be apportioned is not known or easily ascertainable at completion, a provisional apportionment is to be made according to the best estimate available. As soon as the amount is known, a final apportionment is to be made and notified to the other party. Any resulting balance is to be paid no more than ten working days later, and if not then paid the balance is to bear interest at the contract rate from then until payment.

6.3.6 Compensation payable under condition 5.2.6 is not to be apportioned.

6.4   Amount payable

The amount payable by the buyer on completion is the purchase price (less any deposit already paid to the seller or his agent) adjusted to take account of:

(a) apportionments made under condition 6.3

(b) any compensation to be paid or allowed under condition 7.3.

6.5   Title deeds

6.5.1 The seller is not to retain the documents of title after the buyer has tendered the amount payable under condition 6.4.

6.5.2 Condition 6.5.1 does not apply to any documents of title relating to land being retained by the seller after completion.

6.6   Rent receipts

The buyer is to assume that whoever gave any receipt for a payment of rent or service charge which the seller produces was the person or the agent of the person then entitled to that rent or service charge.

6.7   Means of payment

The buyer is to pay the money due on completion in one or more of the following ways:

(a) legal tender

(b) a banker's draft

(c) a direct credit to a bank account nominated by the seller's solicitor

(d) an unconditional release of a deposit held by a stakeholder.

6.8   Notice to complete

6.8.1 At any time on or after completion date, a party who is ready able and willing to complete may give the other a notice to complete.

6.8.2 A party is ready able and willing:

(a) if he could be, but for the default of the other party, and

(b) in the case of the seller, even though a mortgage remains secured on the property, if the amount to be paid on completion enables the property to be transferred freed of all mortgages (except those to which the sale is expressly subject).

6.8.3 The parties are to complete the contract within ten working days of giving a notice to complete, excluding the day on which the notice is given. For this purpose, time is of the essence of the contract.

6.8.4 On receipt of a notice to complete:

(a) if the buyer paid no deposit, he is forthwith to pay a deposit of 10 per cent

(b) if the buyer paid a deposit of less than 10 per cent, he is forthwith to pay a further deposit equal to the balance of that 10 per cent.

7   REMEDIES

7.1   Errors and omissions

7.1.1 If any plan or statement in the contract, or in the negotiations leading to it, is or was misleading or inaccurate due to an error or omission, the remedies available are as follows.

7.1.2 When there is a material difference between the description or value of the property as represented and as it is, the injured party is entitled to damages.

7.1.3 An error or omission only entitles the injured party to rescind the contract:

(a) where it results from fraud or recklessness, or

(b) where he would be obliged, to his prejudice, to transfer or accept property differing substantially (in quantity, quality or tenure) from what the error or omission had led him to expect.

7.2   Rescission

If either party rescinds the contract:

(a) unless the rescission is a result of the buyer's breach of contract the deposit is to be repaid to the buyer with accrued interest

(b) the buyer is to return any documents he received from the seller and is to cancel any registration of the contract.

7.3   Late completion

7.3.1   If there is default by either or both of the parties in performing their obligations under the contract and completion is delayed, the party whose total period of default is the greater is to pay compensation to the other party.

7.3.2   Compensation is calculated at the contract rate on the purchase price, or (where the buyer is the paying party) the purchase price less any deposit paid, for the period by which the paying party's default exceeds that of the receiving party, or, if shorter, the period between completion date and actual completion.

7.3.3   Any claim for loss resulting from delayed completion is to be reduced by any compensation paid under this contract.

7.3.4   Where the buyer holds the property as tenant of the seller and completion is delayed, the seller may give notice to the buyer, before the date of actual completion, that he intends to take the net income from the property until completion. If he does so, he cannot claim compensation under condition 7.3.1 as well.

7.4   After completion

Completion does not cancel liability to perform any outstanding obligation under this contract.

7.5   Buyer's failure to comply with notice to complete

7.5.1   If the buyer fails to complete in accordance with a notice to complete, the following terms apply.

7.5.2   The seller may rescind the contract, and if he does so:

(a) he may

(i)   forfeit and keep any deposit and accrued interest

(ii) resell the property

(iii) claim damages

(b) the buyer is to return any documents he received from the seller and is to cancel any registration of the contract.

7.5.3   The seller retains his other rights and remedies.

7.6   *Seller's failure to comply with notice to complete*

7.6.1   If the seller fails to complete in accordance with a notice to complete, the following terms apply.

7.6.2   The buyer may rescind the contract, and if he does so:

(a) the deposit is to be repaid to the buyer with accrued interest

(b) the buyer is to return any documents he received from the seller and is, at the seller's expense, to cancel any registration of the contract.

7.6.3   The buyer retains his other rights and remedies.

8.   LEASEHOLD PROPERTY

8.1   *Existing leases*

8.1.1   The following provisions apply to a sale of leasehold land.

8.1.2   The seller having provided the buyer with copies of the documents embodying the lease terms, the buyer is treated as entering into the contract knowing and fully accepting those terms.

8.1.3   The seller is to comply with any lease obligations requiring the tenant to insure the property.

8.2   *New leases*

8.2.1   The following provisions apply to a grant of a new lease.

8.2.2   The conditions apply so that:

'seller' means the proposed landlord

'buyer' means the proposed tenant

'purchase price' means the premium to be paid on the grant of a lease.

8.2.3   The lease is to be in the form of the draft attached to the agreement.

8.2.4   If the term of the new lease will exceed 21 years, the seller is to deduce a title which will enable the buyer to register the lease at HM Land Registry with an absolute title.

8.2.5   The buyer is not entitled to transfer the benefit of the contract.

8.2.6   The seller is to engross the lease and a counterpart of it and is to send the counterpart to the buyer at least five working days before completion date.

8.2.7   The buyer is to execute the counterpart and deliver it to the seller on completion.

8.3   *Landlord's consent*

8.3.1   The following provisions apply if a consent to assign or sub-let is required to complete the contract.

8.3.2   (a) The seller is to apply for the consent at his expense, and to use all reasonable efforts to obtain it

(b) The buyer is to provide all information and references reasonably required.

8.3.3   The buyer is not entitled to transfer the benefit of the contract.

8.3.4   Unless he is in breach of his obligation under condition 8.3.2, either party may rescind the contract by notice to the other party if three working days before completion date:

(a) the consent has not been given or

(b) the consent has been given subject to a condition to which the buyer reasonably objects.

In that case, neither party is to be treated as in breach of contract and condition 7.2 applies.

9. CHATTELS

9.1   The following provisions apply to any chattels which are to be sold.

9.2   Whether or not a separate price is to be paid for the chattels, the contract takes effect as a contract for sale of goods.

9.3   Ownership of the chattels passes to the buyer on actual completion.

Index

Criminal Justice and Penology Textbook

**Michael Doherty, BA, MA Criminology,
Senior Lecturer in Law, University of Glamorgan**

An up-to-date and well illustrated account of the key stages of the criminal justice system is provided. The text analyses a plethora of areas relating to the imposition of punitive measures upon criminals in modern English society, including: an exploration of the prospects for crime prevention, evaluation of the role of the police and examination of bail and prosecution decisions. No stage or aspect of the system is left untouched.

What is the impact of the jury system and what is it's importance today? What are the factors that influence sentencing decisions in English courtrooms? How do courts decide between the use of custodial and non-custodial measures? What is the role of prisons and do they fulfil that purpose? A comprehensive and thought-provoking text which encourages its readers to think much more deeply about the philosophies that lie behind the criminal justice system.

For further information on contents or to place an order, please contact:

Mail Order
Old Bailey Press
200 Greyhound Road
London
W14 9RY

Telephone No: 020 7385 3377
Fax No: 020 7381 3377

ISBN 1 85836 372 1
Soft cover 246 x 175 mm
272 pages   £11.95
Due September 2000

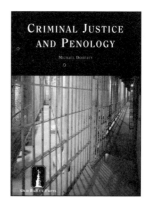

Criminal Justice and Penology Textbook

Michael Doherty, BA, MA (Cantab)
Senior Lecturer in Law, University of Glamorgan

Law Update 2000

Law Update 2001 edition – due February 2001

An annual review of the most recent developments in specific legal subject areas, useful for law students at degree and professional levels, others with law elements in their courses and also practitioners seeking a quick update.

Published around February every year, the Law Update summarises the major legal developments during the course of the previous year. In conjunction with Old Bailey Press textbooks it gives the student a significant advantage when revising for examinations.

Contents

Administrative Law • Civil and Criminal Procedure • Commercial Law • Company Law • Conflict of Laws • Constitutional Law • Contract Law • Conveyancing • Criminal Law • Criminology • English Legal System • Equity and Trusts • European Union Law • Evidence • Family Law • Jurisprudence • Land Law • Law of International Trade • Public International Law • Revenue Law • Succession • Tort

For further information on contents or to place an order, please contact:

Mail Order
Old Bailey Press
200 Greyhound Road
London
W14 9RY

Telephone No: 020 7385 3377
Fax No: 020 7381 3377

ISBN 1 85836 347 0
Soft cover 246 x 175 mm
392 pages   £9.95
Published February 2000

Old Bailey Press

The Old Bailey Press integrated student law library is tailor-made to help you at every stage of your studies from the preliminaries of each subject through to the final examination. The series of Textbooks, Revision WorkBooks, 150 Leading Cases/Casebooks and Cracknell's Statutes are interrelated to provide you with a comprehensive set of study materials.

You can buy Old Bailey Press books from your University Bookshop, your local Bookshop, direct using this form, or you can order a free catalogue of our titles from the address shown overleaf.

The following subjects each have a Textbook, 150 Leading Cases/Casebook, Revision WorkBook and Cracknell's Statutes unless otherwise stated.

Administrative Law
Commercial Law
Company Law
Conflict of Laws
Constitutional Law
Conveyancing (Textbook and Casebook)
Criminal Law
Criminology (Textbook and Sourcebook)
English and European Legal Systems
Equity and Trusts
Evidence
Family Law
Jurisprudence: The Philosophy of Law (Textbook, Sourcebook and
    Revision WorkBook)
Land: The Law of Real Property
Law of International Trade
Law of the European Union
Legal Skills and System
Obligations: Contract Law
Obligations: The Law of Tort
Public International Law
Revenue Law (Textbook,
    Sourcebook and Revision
    WorkBook)
Succession

Mail order prices:	
Textbook	£11.95
150 Leading Cases/Casebook	£9.95
Revision WorkBook	£7.95
Cracknell's Statutes	£9.95
Suggested Solutions 1998–1999	£6.95
Law Update 2000	£9.95
The Practitioner's Handbook 2000	£54.95

To complete your order, please fill in the form below:

Module	Books required	Quantity	Price	Cost
		Postage		
		TOTAL		

For Europe, add 15% postage and packing (£20 maximum).
For the rest of the world, add 40% for airmail.

ORDERING

By telephone to Mail Order at 020 7385 3377, with your credit card to hand.

By fax to 020 7381 3377 (giving your credit card details).

By post to:

Mail Order, Old Bailey Press, 200 Greyhound Road, London W14 9RY.

When ordering by post, please enclose full payment by cheque or banker's draft, or complete the credit card details below. You may also order a free catalogue of our complete range of titles from this address.

We aim to despatch your books within 3 working days of receiving your order.

Name

Address

Postcode   Telephone

Total value of order, including postage: £

I enclose a cheque/banker's draft for the above sum, or

charge my   ☐ Access/Mastercard   ☐ Visa   ☐ American Express
Card number

☐☐☐☐ ☐☐☐☐ ☐☐☐☐ ☐☐☐☐

Expiry date   ☐☐☐☐

Signature: ....Date: ....